Twentieth Century Symphony

By

CHRISTOPHER BALLANTINE

LONDON:
DENNIS DOBSON

First published in Great Britain in 1983
by Dobson Books Ltd, Brancepeth Castle, Durham DH7 8DF

Filmset by Computacomp (UK) Limited, Fort William
Printed by Photobooks (Bristol) Ltd
Barton Manor, St. Philips, Bristol BS2 0RN

ISBN 0 234 72042 5

THE STUDENT'S MUSIC LIBRARY—
HISTORICAL AND CRITICAL SERIES
Edited by
PERCY M. YOUNG

Twentieth Century Symphony

TO SCILLA

Contents

Copyright Acknowledgements

For permission to reproduce musical examples, acknowledgement is gratefully made to the following:

Anglo-Soviet Music Press Ltd.
Boosey & Hawkes Music Publishers Ltd.
Breitkopf & Härtel (London) Ltd.
J. & W. Chester/Edition Wilhelm Hansen (London) Ltd.
Engstrøm & Sødring Musikforlag
Oxford University Press
Peters Edition Limited
Robert Lienau, Berlin
Samfundet Til Udgivelse af Dansk Musik
G. Schirmer Ltd., London
Schott & Co. Ltd.
Universal Edition (Alfred A. Kalmus Ltd.)
Universal Edition (London) Ltd.

Introduction

This study grew out of a wish to provide a first step towards a theoretical understanding of the nature of the symphony in the twentieth century. I know of no book, in any language, which deals with this topic. Mine is therefore the first intensive published investigation in what is a vast, largely unknown, and almost wholly uncharted territory; and as such it will inevitably suffer from the limitations of a pioneer study. As such, too, it is only an attempt: a first contribution to the understanding of the relationship of present to past in a traditional musical field, where that field is at its broadest *defined by the word symphony*. The examination only of pieces explicitly called "symphony" is a necessary delimitation. But by imposing this restriction I do not imply that general symphonic (or sonata) principles are not at work elsewhere; nor that these principles did not from the very beginning give rise to, and influence, forms and styles not explicitly called "symphony".

Inevitably this book will disappoint those who require of it what it does not set out to offer. In particular, it does not attempt to be comprehensive in any sense. It does not attempt to write a history. It does not attempt to mention, let alone discuss, all the symphonies written in our century: it is impossible even to say how many there are, though certainly they are to be numbered in figures over a thousand rather than in scores or hundreds; in fact I discuss less than one hundred of them. And it does not attempt to give exhaustive analyses of the particular works dealt with.

While many more works were studied than are actually dealt with here—indeed a vast number of works had to be exhaustively analysed in the first instance—I have tried to discuss *only* those works that seemed to me to be

11

representative of a trend, or to bear an otherwise significant relationship to the symphonic tradition. But I do not claim to have dealt with all, or even most, works that might be considered representative or significant. Some inclusions may surprise, some omissions may surprise as much. However, to avoid a very likely misunderstanding, it should be stressed that the fact that a work is included or excluded does not carry implications for its value as a piece of music, or even as a symphony. A relatively unknown work, or even one not usually considered important, might be cited as well as one of accepted importance, if the unknown or "unimportant" work is able to tell us something about what a symphony is or might be in the twentieth century. Besides, our "established" contemporary hierarchies, musical and otherwise, are notoriously poor indicators as to what the really dynamic and original processes at work are. In general, I have not tried to justify an inclusion (or an omission) as a separate undertaking. In a field so large that it soon stretches beyond the bounds of the knowable, and even sooner becomes unmanageable, there can logically be no *absolute* justification for my choices: the points that emerge from the discussions of these choices are themselves implicitly the only—if partial—justification for what I have included, and what left out. The absence of a little-known work may mean simply that I did not know of its existence; the absence of a well-known work probably means that its inclusion would have added nothing very much to the argument: it is this latter that explains that absence of, for instance, even a mention of the symphonic oeuvre of Roussel. It seemed to me as I pursued my researches that the best way—the only way— to make preliminary sense of so vast and so unknown a territory was to explore something of both the relatively familiar and the unfamiliar, moving from the one to the other; to plot a course around various recognizable landmarks and, resisting the temptation to stay always where it is safe, to begin excursions into the outlying terrain. The discussion of works of very differing fame and stature is therefore a conscious methodological feature of this study.

Thus Chapter 1, as a summary dealing with well-charted

pre-twentieth-century territory, attempts to lay the groundwork for the main part of the book by making brief comment on a number of pertinent issues. It establishes a necessary frame of reference. The rest of the book isolates only certain aspects of the works dealt with, in order to indicate trends, or matters of significance, in a hitherto largely *un*charted territory: these are implicitly or explicitly related to that frame of reference. I repeat that there is no attempt at a comprehensive picture of each work. Indeed, the discussions of individual works rest on a purposeful limitation. Since in the historical period under review the symphony has undergone radical changes, my eye has been fixed throughout on the shifting relation between technique and something that I take to be symphonic "essence". As such mine is a quest for more than technique. Inevitably, of course, the discussion leads into a consideration of technique—but *only* of such techniques (whether form or tonality, etc.) as happen *at that moment* to be relevant to the discussion.

In addition, then, to the general restriction that only works actually titled symphony are considered, another limitation—which I implied by the term "symphonic essence"—is sustained throughout this study, and one that will account for the absence of at least a few works from its pages. It is that since the symphony (as will be shown) first came to life as the large-scale incarnation and exploration of musical dualism,[1] and developed as such in its nineteenth-century mainstream, I have taken this musical preoccupation with dualism (and with the dialectic that accommodates it) to be an essential symphonic characteristic and one whose embodiment in twentieth-century works called "symphony" not only serves to define our field, but also—where the dualistic *technique* is quite novel—demands of us fresh responses and new modes of analysis.

The large-scale exploration of dualism, then, has been seen as a condition of genuine symphonic thought. By implication, there may be (and indeed are—in our century more frequently than in the last) works called symphony that do not meet this condition. It is important to stress that since this emphasis on musical duality is a *categorical* and not a *normative* criterion, the fact of a work's being outside the symphonic tradition—whether that work is called symphony or not—has no necessary bearing on our estimation of it as a musical work. Some composers, quite simply, have used the word symphony at the head of a piece in the absence of a better word—sometimes because superficially the word seems to fit. Of course, a composer may try to write a symphony and fail. But in any event it is not *in itself* the presence or absence of the willingness of a work to pursue some musically meaningful dualism that would enable us to praise or condemn it. In every case the work should itself suggest the criteria by which it must be judged. Once this is understood, it will be clear that one takes nothing away from (for example) Britten's *Spring Symphony* by saying that, in an essential traditional sense of the term, it is not a symphony at all. The logic of the *Spring Symphony* is that of its text; the work seems to owe less to the tradition of the symphony than to that of the English oratorio. Much the same could be said of Vaughan Williams's *Sea Symphony*, its use of more orthodox symphonic forms notwithstanding. Examples of a different kind are the Third, Fourth and Fifth Symphonies of Henze, in which an interest in static sonorities is primary; Rubbra's Fifth Symphony, which is a work of pure contrapuntal monism (and as such is typical of his symphonic output); Vaughan Williams's *London Symphony*, in which the sonata form basically "arranges" the folk tunes; or his *Pastoral Symphony*, which is a kind of impressionistic rhapsody, its climaxes owing nothing to conflict.

A more explicit note on method will not be out of place here. There would appear two main ways in which a book devoted to a theoretical understanding of the twentieth-century symphony might be written. The first possibility is that the discussion be organized on the basis of "obvious" distinctions and similarities between symphonies, composers, etc. For example, one might order the discussion chronologically, or perhaps group works under headings reflecting their country of origin. This might be called a "sequential" organization. The disadvantage of this approach is that since the field of study is so enormously complex and so little explored, the only "obvious" or evidently "innate" headings are the most superficial ones.

The second possibility is what might be called a "thematic" organization; and it is this method I have adopted in the main portion of the work. I have tried to reveal a more profound and meaningful order in this huge, intractable twentieth-century field by organizing the discussion on the basis of symphonic forms and procedures which are

(a) inferentially related to the symphonic tradition, and
(b) studied in rational relation to each other.

Hence the following outline of the book is arrived at.

Chapter 1 (constituting Part One of the book) is a fairly lengthy—and indispensable—"review", establishing historical categories, concepts, etc., as well as setting down the main lines of development in the symphony before Mahler. The discussion of twentieth-century symphonies begins after this: the two following chapters move logically through *formal* developments in the twentieth-century symphony; together they constitute Part Two of the book. Thus Chapter 2 discusses "moderate" departures from (historically) orthodox form; i.e. innovations clearly based on or derived from earlier symphonic practice. And Chapter 3 deals with radical formal innovations; i.e. where features historically associated with the symphony are obscured or even annihilated.

The last two sections of the book, Chapters 4 and 5 (constituting Part Three), deal specifically with new procedures (i.e. other than the historical opposition of themes and keys) for incarnating symphonic dualism: procedures whose invention has been made *necessary* by the stylistic, linguistic, and formal developments in twentieth-century music.

My enquiry indirectly raises a number of important questions. One of the most pressing of these is the question why the changes that I describe came about at all. I need hardly reiterate that it is no part of my purpose to answer these in the present book. If the beginning of Chapter 1 does propose socio-historic foundations for the rise of the sonata principle, this is for no other reason than to give a solid grounding to the quintessential sonata principle of dualism and dialectic, and to give a concrete historical basis to the argument that there grew up a specific symphonic tradition distinct from other musical traditions. But I would add that any questions so raised are part of the general area of enquiry that my essay may have opened up, and which I hope others may feel inclined to enter. The area is vast, and the questions insistent.

NOTE

[1] The term has been used by many music historians in connection with the sonata principle: I use it in the same sense as they do. See for instance Lang, P. H.; *Music in Western Civilisation*, p. 590 ff; and Mellers, Wilfrid; *Man and his Music*, p. 587 ff. This use of the term has nothing whatever to do with the "harmonic dualism" of Zarlino, Rameau, Riemann and others.

Part One

Before the Twentieth Century:
Concepts, Categories, Evolution

I

The Symphony before Mahler: a brief retrospect

I

The rise of the symphony in the eighteenth century corresponds with, among other things, the rise of democracy and of the tradition of Hegelian dialectical thought. There is a strong connection between these. In the early eighteenth century none of the prevalent musical forms was capable of representing society in all its contradictory complexity, though the sum of the forms and styles loosely did so. Moreover each of the forms was monistic in the sense that it was grounded on a single centre (a tonality, a thematic complex, a rhythmic predisposition), the full diversification of which constituted the piece.

The symphony—and the sonata principle in general—began to take from the pre-existing forms and to forge a new single form; of the sum it made a synthetic unity; and the monistic control of a single centre gave way to the dualisms of opposing tonalities, themes, rhythmic characters, within the course of a single movement as well as over a multi-movement structure. Further, the baroque principle of instrumental registration yielded to the instrumental democracy of the symphony orchestra and the individualistic, soloistic liberty of the players in it. The *Affektenlehre* fell under the attack of Rousseau and the *Sturm und Drang*; the terraced dynamics of the Baroque were usurped by the sweep of the Mannheim crescendo. There was free speech—and the dramatic argument and flux of sonata development. The old order, which was God- or State-centred, and hegemonic, was surpassed by the new, which hoped to be rationalistic, liberal, universal and democratic. Late feudalism crumbled under the pressure of

19

the revolutionary forces in society. What was generally happening, in Hegelian terms, was that the contradictory viewpoints which carried forward, and resisted, the social changes, were transcended by and conserved in the higher synthetic unity represented by the new democratic order.

The musical analogue of this process was the rise of the sonata principle, in which the dualistically opposed tonal centres and their attendant paraphernalia came to suggest antithetical "world-views",[1] and the total work their synthetic resolution. Philip Barford has also remarked on this analogy:

> It is a highly thought-provoking fact that the rise and establishment of the sonata-principle corresponded in the most intimate way with the gradual emergence and full flowering of a comprehensive metaphysical system which, in so many respects, is the ultimate rationale of the logic of the sonata-principle ... The Hegelian system, at its finest, is a superb justification of the sonata-principle. Similarly, the classical sonata, at its finest, is a sensuous embodiment of the dialectical relationship of opposed terms. In the collective consciousness of late eighteenth-century man, some vital force was at work which found expression in music, literature and philosophy—in Haydn, Mozart and Beethoven, in Goethe, in Hegel. It was the same force. It found diverse expressions.[2]

II

By the 1760's the symphony stood unchallenged as the highest form of instrumental music. Its achievement of this position coincides with the earliest date we can give to the birth of the symphonic tradition that runs through Haydn, Mozart, and Beethoven, to Mahler and beyond: the composers of the *Sturm und Drang* deepened the *galant* symphony into something of greater human importance, and they wrote into it a principle of integration whereby each element had implications that were to be fully explored and realized in the context of the whole, which was greater than the sum of the parts. Hiller, writing of the "new symphonies" about the same time, makes it clear that the concept of dualism was not the invention of later theorists trying to be wise after the event, even if for contemporary musicians it was sometimes a "problem":

> ... It is true that one can find some well written, beautiful and effective movements among them ... but the strange mixture of the serious and the comical, the sublime and the lowly, which so frequently is blended in the same movement, often creates a bad effect.[3]

And a few years earlier, in 1753, C. P. E. Bach had said: "Hardly has the executant musician stilled one emotion than he excites another; thus does he juggle with the passions."

The growth of the symphony towards its condition of the last third of the eighteenth century had been surprisingly rapid in view of the many and radical changes that had had to be effected. Around mid-century lay one of the great and—now, as then—least documented watersheds of Western musical history, perfectly symbolized by the death of J. S. Bach in 1750. It was not much before 1730 that the *sinfonia* began to be composed independently, instead of *avanti l'opera*, with Sammartini and other Italians leading the way and German, French, and Austrian composers following. The fast-slow-fast scheme of movements supplied the basic shape of the piece; the genesis had (democratically) involved a good deal else by the time men such as Stamitz had added a fourth movement and the various movements' origins had to be traced respectively to the *buffo* overture, the operatic aria, the dance suite, and either *buffo* (binary) or dance (rondo) styles. When fugue was adapted to the new instrumental form, or when Haydn prefixed a first movement with a slow introduction that was *only* introduction, refining his—and Georg Monn's—earlier practice of writing a whole slow first movement in the *da chiesa* manner, the origins could be still more diverse, the synthesis yet more remarkable. The gradual definition of dualistically contrasting key-areas in the first movement grew from the binary dance forms' habit of moving to the dominant (or relative major) before the double-bar; the tendency in the Baroque concerto to enhance with contrasting figuration its vertical and horizontal differentiation between "ripieno" and "concertino" lent a thematic emphasis to this development just as Vivaldi's episodes gave some precedent for a transition between the groups.[4] Rinaldo di Capua, by hinting at a secondary thematic area, Sammartini by being probably the first to grasp the hint and write a second subject or group, and Stamitz, by helping to make it standard practice, were key figures in this connection. The necessary modulation after the double-bar in the binary dance form gave the foundation to what soon became recognizable as the symphony's development section. But the notion of modulation was foremost. At first there was no development: Sammartini, for instance, would merely play his first subject again, in the dominant. By the time C. P. E. Bach was concerning himself with development, however, that section might be the dramatic central section of the movement. In a rounded binary form, after the modulation back to the tonic, some recollection of the opening would follow; the principle of recapitulation was latent here—as it was more obviously, if less meaningfully for the symphony, in the *da capo* aria. And the idea of re-entrenchment of the tonic was primary, and thematic reprise only secondary, as is borne out by the fact that in many pre-classical symphonic recapitulations the original thematic material was recalled only in part or under some species of radical variation, while the tonic invariably came round again.

One of the great and absolutely necessary achievements of the new musical order in the eighteenth century was the invention of a new kind of melodic forming and generation, a new kind of movement, a grammar; the dualistic style, sustaining dynamic motion and a large structure and integrating thematic contrasts, is unthinkable without it. Baroque melody had been virtually superseded by influences from folk and operatic sources; in the absence of the Baroque "motor" and of the *melos* that invited progress by the principle of continuity, one of the great problems of the early or pre-Classical composers was "how to go on". Their problem was as acute as their breathless cadences were frequent. Their solution was the invention of what Schoenberg called the method of developing variation—and what Reti[5] called the technique of trans-formation. Wagenseil, Stamitz, and others—vesting the periodized symphonic themes with a kinetic motivic signifi-cance—and Haydn—especially in the "Russian" quartets—mark roughly the points of incipience and fulfilment in the development of this technique.

A few general observations on some differences in grammar between the old order and the new might be pertinent here, since an understanding of the differences is crucial to any account of the sonata principle. And the differences are of degree rather than kind: Schoenberg characterized the new syntax as depending in part on "a more elaborated development through variations of the motive";[6] and Reti stated the matter as follows:

> ... while imitation strove to this height [in Palestrina, Lassus, and others], the other principle, variation, was by no means discarded. Yet it did not at that time progress to as comprehensive and methodical an art of structural formation as did imitation. It rather remained at the comparatively simple stage that it had reached a few centuries before. No definite system, no concrete *technique of thematic varying* was yet developed. This decisive step from a simple stage of varying to an elaborate, subtle technique was not taken until the thematic, the classical style superseded the contrapuntal. This more elaborate, more complex method of varying a given shape we call *transformation.*[7]

In music of the contrapuntal era each statement, motive, etc., insofar as one can isolate it at all, is followed by another which is closely connected and which yields up some of its implications—almost as though the two were one or in a relationship of some kind of organic growth. In music of the sonata era each statement, motive, etc., is followed by one which diversifies the original, as though the relationship were more or less tenuous—but which reveals a close identity *at a deeper level.* "In the contrapuntal style", said Schoenberg,

> the theme is practically unchangeable and all the necessary contrasts are produced by the addition of one or more voices. Homophony produces all its contrasts by developing variation.[8]

In philosophical terms, the older principle may be described as monistic and analytic, the other as dualistic, dialectical, and synthetic. As for theme so for harmony, a dyad whose parts are, strictly, inseparable: it is much more true of music of the sonata era than of the contrapuntal that each harmonic step forward brings with it a crucial imbalance so that it stands in need of reintegration. Paradoxically, in the best music each thematic and harmonic step forward also brings with it simultaneously its own partial, *deeper*, reintegration: this is what we mean by logic. Small imbalances find their full reintegration on the nearest adequate dialectical plane—say the period or paragraph; the large imbalances or contradictions are the contrasting subject-groups, the opposed tonalities, and then the various movements, and these will find equilibrium only in the context of their whole—the movement or the whole work. (This is what Furtwängler meant when he said[9] that in Haydn musical unity had to be striven for—and that this was the starting point of modern music).

The terms "dynamic" and "static" are often used to differentiate roughly between music that participates in the sense of movement peculiar to sonata, and music that does not; the terms are useful for they make a fundamental distinction. Riezler's use of the terms may make their function, and some of the related points we have been discussing, more clear:

> Bach's music is complete from the very beginning, and in essence remains unchanged, whatever may befall it as it runs its course. The theme of a passacaglia, a fugue, or any apparently freely constructed composition of Bach, is fixed and constant in form from the very first, and is, in its essence, unchanged even by inversion, augmentation

and so forth ... And what happens round about the theme is predetermined by its shape and kind. This is "static" form—form that is a fixed condition and not a process ... And the feeling that is in this music is also static.[10]

Sonata form, on the other hand,

is a dynamic form, which does not, like the static fugue, merely unfold what was already there, but gradually develops its own essential substance, travelling a road whose end was not to be foreseen at the beginning.[11]

And the following quotation from Furtwängler restates the case in other terms, with an important emphasis on *theme*:

The decisive factor which was introduced into the history of music by Haydn and which became a complete reality in Beethoven's work, was that the subject should develop organically within the work, like a Shakespearean character. With Bach, the entire potential development of a work is implicit in the subject ... each piece runs its predestined course ... But with Beethoven this development is not predetermined solely by the first subject; Beethoven uses several subjects from the opposition and permutation of which the piece develops ... *They have to bear a destiny of own* [my italics].[12]

We are now in a position to begin to consider, first in general terms and later with attention to detail, the growth and fortunes of the symphony up to the end of the nineteenth century. By attempting to deal mainly with the major works of the major symphonic composers, our discussion will try to suggest the principal lines of the symphonic tradition; but it will thus not always move strictly chronologically.

III

If the development in the symphony through the middle of the eighteenth century had been enormous, securing for it a position of pre-eminence by the 1760's, there are a number of senses in which its life during the last third of the century was even more remarkable. Perhaps the most immediately striking is that Haydn and Mozart, inheriting the symphony in what was still basically its Italian *sinfonia* style, freed it finally of its *buffo* limitations and made it a vehicle adequate to their most profound inspirations. Henceforth its composition would be an immense human undertaking. Haydn's own career fully spans this change. His earliest symphonies—up to about 1760—even include the three-movement type and employ terraced dynamics. Soon he introduced the minuet, and began giving depth to the finale; in the *Sturm und Drang* symphonies of the eight-or-so years after 1766 he reached maturity: a sure hand permitted experiments in style and form (e.g. No. 45), and a desire for unity called for connections, sometimes even quotations, between movements. The reactionary symphonies of the next ten years—the Esterházy circle required simplification—were later fully compensated for by the high Classicism, the beautiful integrated structures, of the "Paris" set, and then by the "Salomon" symphonies, all works that could take central rather than peripheral place in a programme. These pieces for London are the summit of his symphonic achievement: like Mozart's last six symphonies they provided the models for a generation and longer. And Haydn's No. 102 is probably the first "dramatic" symphony, inasmuch as it is the first to introduce the idea of full-scale thematic conflict, and the notion of victory.

For Mozart, as for Haydn, C. P. E. Bach was one starting-point—though Mozart was also influenced at least as much by J. C. Bach and Schobert. Mozart's symphonic career began with the light three-movement type in which the first movement was the most important, the second a small cantabile movement (usually andante), and the third a rapid (sometimes minuet-) finale. But around 1773—about eight years later—Mozart could write three symphonies of astounding individuality, one in the "difficult", anti-*buffo* key of G minor, and exhibiting a new level of thematic unification. This was the time he first heard Haydn's *Sturm und Drang* symphonies, and the experience hastened the change towards intensification and deepening of content that had been evident in his symphonic writing during the preceding years. The amazing unity and structural ingenuity of the last symphonies, anticipated in some senses in the early triad, has been demonstrated by Keller and others: among them are the four or five that Einstein argues are written according to the ideal that held for Beethoven and Brahms—orchestral works "addressed, above and beyond any occasion for [their] composition, to an ideal public, to humanity."[13] The extent of this achievement must appear the more remarkable when the symphony's Baroque genesis becomes once more suddenly apparent—as it does in the *Prague* (and often in Haydn) where on the analogy of the Baroque concerto the first subject in the exposition is played again, in the dominant, before the entry of the second subject.

Beethoven, indeed, found in those late, great works of Mozart his most powerful precedents. But while for Mozart, and for Haydn, it had been normally sufficient that the dualistic tendencies of a symphony be contained by being felicitously balanced, for Beethoven the dualistic principle became to a far greater degree a means of playing out a drama of the emotions: what had been a neat contrast of keys, themes, sections, and movements, in subtle and intricate dialectical syntheses, became for him a means of dramatic presentation and ultimate reconciliation of conflicting modes of experience: the symphony became an analogue of the experience of Becoming. And Beethoven understood very well (as the late works in particular so miraculously show) that there could conceivably be ways of organizing a logical working-out of the dualistic principle that were not contingent upon this kind of first movement, or that number of distinct sections, or certain key relationships. Now the implications of this potential in the sonata principle for adaptation and renewal, though imperfectly understood for the better part of the nineteenth century, were ultimately enormous, as we shall see during the course of this study.

Beethoven's extension of the notion of universal sonata-dualism into a concept involving *conflict* also had towering, and troublesome, implications for his successors. And not only for his successors: "Two principles!" he insisted in one of his manifestos. "A thousand musicians fail to comprehend this!" Certainly his dualistic contrasts shocked and baffled his contemporaries: a correspondent of the *Freymüthige* who was at the first performance of the *Eroica* reported of a faction of the audience that it

> denies that the work has any artistic value ... By means of strange moods and violent transitions, by combining the most heterogeneous elements ... a certain undesirable originality may be achieved without much trouble.[14]

Even in 1862, when Berlioz published his commentary on Beethoven's symphonies in Paris, there was still the need to defend the onslaught of the beginning of the finale in the Fifth Symphony against critics who, he wrote,

> tried to detract from the merit of the composer by declaring that ... he had resorted to a mere vulgar procedure; the brightness of the major mode pompously succeeding the obscurity of the minor *pianissimo*.[15]

Along with the intensification of contrasts, Beethoven evolved brilliant means for their resolution, leading specifically—for this is what mattered to him—to the idea of symphonic triumph. Reti has dealt fully with the species known as thematic resolution;[16] we need only remind ourselves here of the core of his argument:

> Beethoven's "thematic resolutions" have almost in-variably one characteristic in common: structurally they transform a shape which has a quality of discord into an expression of perfect harmony. For instance, a line centred around a chord of the seventh is resolved into a triad, or a complex chordal progression into one rooted in the tonic-dominant relation. Correspondingly, in the dramatic-emotional sense Beethoven's resolutions lead from tension to release, from compulsion to liberation, from the tragic to the joyous ...
> In almost all of his symphonies we see the opening

Allegro theme at the end of the movement changed into a shape of resolved discord, of released tension.[17]

Beethoven's contrasts, if intensified, also used motives which were extramusical and dramatic, as Salazar has said, unlike those of Classicism which were "as explicit as two-plus-two".[18] At its most vulgar this change could lead to the crass, blatant programmaticism of the *Battle* Symphony, where the oppositions of *Rule Britannia* and *Malbrough s'en-va-t-en-guerre* represent the struggle between the English and the French; at its most sublime to the metaphysical symbols of the Ninth Symphony. The difference here is one of degree: new, and common to both, is the manifest preoccupation with a dialectic of *conflict*, a dualism now specific rather than universal in the Classical manner: Beethoven, said Reti, would not have rejected allegorical interpretations. But with these developments came a threat to symphonic unity, already endangered by a widening of the tonal orbit and his expansion of the symphonic structure, the latter made possible partly by his slowing down of harmonic tempo. The Sixth Symphony is his final symphonic exploitation of the architectonic capabilities of the Classical tonal system;[19] and his tendency towards the *kolossal*, a Romantic urge that was to find its fulfilment in the huge works of Bruckner and Mahler, culminates in the Ninth Symphony. Beethoven answered the threat to unity by tightening the network of motives and binding the movements together. The cyclic motto in the Fifth Symphony was radical in its time; and in that work and in the Ninth Symphony parts of a previous movement are recalled in the finale, while in the Fifth and Sixth Symphonies some movements are literally bound together. We shall also see the implications of these innovations.

In Schubert we already have a symphonic "problem". "What more can be done?" he asked. His question, at once humble and indignant, speaks for every serious symphonist who happened to live in the shadow of Beethoven—and that means almost every one in the nineteenth century. How the question was answered provides the fascinating symphonic history of that century. But the problem which faced those composers was not just that Beethoven had lived before them: it is also referable to their Romantic predicament. The versatile sonata grammar, the taut dialectical technique, and the established formal articulation—at first simply the means of organizing the principle but now abstracted from former practice and reified into a mould —all these things were no longer immediately relevant to the age, or immediately appropriate to its musical inspirations.

Schubert dealt with Beethoven by avoiding his full implications. Those works that acknowledge him (in general the Second, Fourth, and Sixth Symphonies) refer principally to Beethoven's first two symphonies: in retrospect the first movement of Beethoven's Second Symphony seems in its style and instrumentation particularly (early) Schubertian. The composer knew a good deal of the instrumental music of Haydn and Mozart, including the late symphonies of each; his First, Third, and Fifth Symphonies look back to the older men or their contemporaries. What we feel about all the above symphonies of Schubert is that their form is inherited, a legacy used as a "prop", rather than a deeply structural control. In the Fourth (*Tragic*) Symphony, for instance, the exposition of the first movement has a closing section that is all empty gesture. And in the allegro finale the substitution in the recapitulation of major mode for minor, and the embarrassing heroic histrionics that follow, constitute one of the century's first attempts to simulate a Beethovenian finale of triumph. Moreover, Schubert's kaleidoscopic sense of key and his notoriously recalcitrant song-subjects are a contradiction of sonata function and dynamic *Durchführung*. Only in the last two symphonies are these problems resolved and the symphonic tradition renewed, in a way that was not that of Beethoven or anybody else, but peculiarly his own. He did not banish song but subjugated it to a precise, strictly relevant dramatic role. Harmonic tempo was now slower than ever, precision and economy as telling as ever. From Beethoven he learnt the meaning of conflict, but with Schubert symphonic resolution is achieved not so much by victory as by the kind of affirmation that ultimately rises above conflict.

Schubert's Ninth Symphony is, with Beethoven's, one of the first of the huge nineteenth-century symphonies.

The gradual appearance of anything as precise as the Leipzig school or its neo-German opposition is evidence of a split in the symphonic tradition after Beethoven, inseparable from the Romantic symphonic problem in all its complexity. An important aspect of this split—and therefore of the symphonic problem—is the polarization of different attitudes towards the past in general, as towards Beethoven in particular.

Mendelssohn was the first of the Leipzig composers to attempt to renew the past by creating within it—but he did so only within those aspects of it that he could understand. Like Schubert he avoided some of Beethoven's greatest implications by ignoring them, taking instead for his model, in his finest symphonies, the *Italian* and the *Scotch*, a work such as the *Pastoral* Symphony with its admitted points of inspiration and its relatively unproblematic relation to the eighteenth-century *Musiziersymphonie*. This implied conservative interest in the Classical past is evident in the symphonies for string orchestra which he wrote between 1821 and 1823: those of the twelve that are now available abound in winks at Haydn and Mozart. The Op. 11 of 1824—Mendelssohn's thirteenth symphony and one of the only three symphonies he ever allowed to reach publication—is in a C minor that is pre-Beethovenian (except perhaps for a major-mode conclusion). The *Lobgesang* is surely not a choral symphony on the Beethovenian precedent but a cantata of twelve choral and solo sections preceded by a prologue of three symphonic movements; the similarity with the Ninth Symphony is hardly more than superficial.

Yet despite these dispositions, only rarely—perhaps only once—did Mendelssohn achieve the fine syntheses that had characterized the mainstream of the symphonic tradition before that time. He undermined dynamism by tending to substitute a square thematic periodicity for the vital protoplasmic asymmetricality first perfected by Haydn. The relationship between movements, between sections, became looser, less necessary, and more episodic. The nadir

31

is perhaps the *Reformation* Symphony. At the same time he rendered a contribution in trying to counteract the increasing diffuseness by following up Beethoven's hints about cyclicism, thematic cross-reference, and movement-binding—as in the *Scotch* Symphony for instance, though no amount of stitching can obscure the fact that this is still form *filled out*. Best is the *Italian* Symphony, the most thoroughly "driven" of the symphonies, a work unified by an abiding central concern which now *articulates* form—with startling consequences—and Mendelssohn's only symphony fully to take issue with the Beethovenian ethic of conflict. We shall need to return to it again during this study.

Schumann, as great critic, was his generation's most articulate analyst of the symphonic problem, and—or more correctly, because—he was one of the few who understood the importance of Beethoven's greatest achievements.[20] But he was not optimistic. In 1835 he had "almost feared that the term 'symphony' might soon become a thing of the past"; in 1839 he wrote that "isolated beautiful examples of it [i.e. sonata form] will certainly still be written now and then—and have been written already—but it seems that this form has run its life course". Essentially he was raising the same question as Schubert had done: what more could be done after Beethoven?—

It is so often said, and to the considerable annoyance of composers, that "after Beethoven one should forego symphonic ambitions", and it is true that most of those who have disregarded this advice have produced only lifeless mirrorings of Beethovenian idioms, not to mention those sorry, dull symphonists who have managed a tolerable suggestion of the powdered wigs of Haydn and Mozart but not their heads.[21]

In a review of new symphonies in the *Neue Zeitschrift* in 1839 Schumann examined the problem more fully, criticising contemporary symphonic writing on grounds we have familiarized ourselves with:

When the German talks about symphonies, he speaks of Beethoven. For him the words "symphony" and

"Beethoven" are synonymous and inseparable ...
Beethoven's works having become a part our innermost
being—even certain of the symphonies have become popular—one would assume that they had left deep traces,
and that these would be visible in the works of the succeeding generation, particularly in works of the same
category. Such is not the case. We hear reminiscences, to
be sure, although curiously enough, mostly of the earlier
symphonies, as if each of them required a certain time to
be understood and imitated. Reminiscences there are—
too many and too strong. But mastery of the grand form,
where ideas follow one another in rapid succession,
bound together by an inner spiritual bond, is encountered—with certain exceptions—only rarely. The
newer symphonies level out for the greater part, into the
overture style, particularly the first movements. The slow
movements are there only because custom requires it.
The scherzos are such in name only. The last movements
no longer know what the earlier movements contained.[22]

What then was to be done? On the one hand Schumann
hinted at a solution in the last quotation: one would expect
"deep traces" of the Beethovenian symphony "in the works
of the succeeding generation". On the other, the difference
between the two ages and their musical styles had to be
taken fully into account: as he himself once said, the sonata
style of 1790 is not that of 1840. In a word, "the ideal
modern symphony, which, since Beethoven, has left us,
must necessarily take another direction."
Schumann's four symphonies are his attempt to give that
new direction. The principle is that of conscious renewal,
which we shall encounter repeatedly in the history of the
symphony. Since Beethoven in 1841 could not be avoided
except in bad faith, he had to be accepted: in that year
Schumann began a study of Beethoven's symphonies in
preparation for the writing of his own.
The First (*Spring*) Symphony is, like some of
Mendelssohn's, a relative of the *Pastoral*; the titles to the
movements, openly suggesting the sources of inspiration,
would, even if they had not been suppressed, have made no

difference to the plain truth that this is not programmatic music. The other symphonies similarly have suppressed or undeclared "titles", in the manner of most of Beethoven's. The Second Symphony, while Schumann's most Classical in form, is obviously Beethovenian in the way it grows out of Schumann's self-confessed "fear and struggle against the spectre of madness". Its dramatic life is, as prototypically in Beethoven, expressible in terms of a dualistic conflict which culminates in victory.

The Fourth Symphony is also manifestly of the same kind. It is, moreover, one of the most important in the history of the symphony, and for a number of reasons. One of these we shall touch on immediately: it represents the highest point to which external integration of the symphony within a broadly traditional format had been taken, either in Schumann's work or the work of any other men, and it remained unique throughout the century. The tendency towards integration is generally observable in Schumann's symphonic writing, and it places him in the line that runs through Beethoven and Mendelssohn. There are mottos in the First and Second Symphonies, which do not always disguise the fact that the sectional relationships are, as in Mendelssohn, looser and less telling than formerly.

The Third Symphony (*Rhenish*) goes so far in trying to unify its contrasts, sometimes through simple motivic means, that as a result the contrasts are merely incidental, no longer generative.[23] The Fourth Symphony uses every known external integratory device including that of running the four movements into each other without a break, and inter-movement assimilations; likely sources for some of these devices are the *Wanderer* Fantasy and the *Symphonie Fantastique*. While in general Schumann strove to bind and compress the symphony, unlike many of his contemporaries who continued to expand it, he did not always do so: the *Rhenish* has an extra slow movement, and in the first two symphonies he used two independent trios, as Mozart had done before him.

For all his awareness of Beethoven, Schumann did not succeed in writing a symphony that was fully heir to Beethoven's symphonic legacy. That had to await an heir for half a century, until the 1870's when Brahms and others proclaimed the symphonic renaissance. By a formidable effort of concentration Brahms retrieved the principles, much of the spirit, and a surprising amount of the technique of the Beethoven symphonies. This is not to say that he simply imitated them. His musical idiom is fully contemporary. And he was prepared to differ from Beethoven in such primary matters as metrical schemes, key relationships between movements, and dramatic purpose. None of the first movements is in the usual 4/4 time, and of the twelve remaining movements only two, and a part of a third, are indeed in it. For inter-movement key schemes he generally preferred mediant relationships. Only the First Symphony—in Beethoven's heroic C minor—attempts a genuine apotheosis in the manner of Beethoven in the finale: the others move ever closer to positions of stoical acceptance; and the Third in its time was the only important symphony since Haydn's *Farewell* to conclude softly and diminuendo. At the same time, with only two minor exceptions his orchestra never exceeds that of Beethoven's Ninth Symphony; the exceptions are the tuba in the Second and a third drum in the Fourth Symphony. And his modulatory orbit is closer to Beethoven's than are those of his contemporaries and even his predecessors. He relates to Beethoven at more profound levels, however. He connects immediately and always with the Beethovenian principle of generative conflict; indeed, it was perhaps his over-solicitousness in seeking a dramatic contrast to his first groups that led to the frequently criticised lyrical stereotype of his second groups;[24] but that his second groups carry a powerful dualistic charge is undeniable.

In Brahms's hands the symphony regains its former dynamic sense of movement and direction; phrases and cells boil over, obliterating squareness. And the symphony is once again a perfect synthesis, single, stable, complete—and "written in its own length", to use a phrase of Tovey's. Eschewing the external integratory devices of his Romantic predecessors, Brahms unifies internally. His subtle unifications through the Classical principle of thematic transformation and through motivic allusion cannot be called "mottos"—as they sometimes are—without doing violence to their nature. To find that the "rationale" of the second subject of the finale of the Second Symphony is that it includes a "motto-figure" is to overlook the fact that, as Reti has demonstrated,[25] it is really a synthesis of all the thematic impulses of the symphony, and is thus a thematic resolution in the finest Beethovenian tradition.

We must now return to the time of Beethoven's death to trace the development of symphonists who moved in quite another direction from the one we have been considering. We shall find that the men in this loosely defined tradition also took Beethoven as their immediate starting point; regarding themselves in their own way as disciples of Beethoven, they set out to continue this symphonic line. If their work led them into what may look like surprisingly new territory we shall see that this was as much because they meant to realize to the full Beethoven's implications, as because they were less reverent.

Indeed, Berlioz is supposed once to have said to Fétis: "I took up music where Beethoven left it." In the spring of 1828, shortly before the start of his symphonic career, he attended Habeneck's performance of Beethoven's symphonies for the *Société des Concerts* in Paris. The effect on him was overwhelming:

> I had scarcely recovered from the visions of Shakespeare and Weber when I beheld Beethoven's giant form looming above the horizon. The shock was almost as great as that I had received from Shakespeare, and a new world of music was revealed to me by the musician, just as a new universe of poetry had been opened to me by the poet.[26]

But never was there any apology in the admission of his differences from orthodox practice:

> I never dreamt of making music *without melody*, as so many in France are stupid enough to say. Such a school now exists in Germany, and I hold it in detestation. It is easy to see that, without confining myself to a short air from the theme of the piece, as the great masters often do, I have

always taken care that my compositions shall be rich in melody.[27]

Later he made an intensive study of the symphonies of Beethoven. The influence may in some ways even have been harmful to him, as Tom Wotton has suggested:[28] hailed as a successor to Beethoven, he may have felt bound to justify the connection by complying with Teutonic criteria that were irrelevant to his style. Only seldom, however, does this amount to a disparity between means and ends. The *Symphonie Fantastique*, arriving so soon after the symphonic achievements of high Classicism, comes to proclaim a new "world", quite unlike anything in the genre before it; as immediately French, as un-Viennese, almost as "felt", as Debussy, the first movement nevertheless accepts the Classical heritage in dynamically and individualistically *using* sonata form and coming to terms with the principle of dramatic dualism. These, and the way the whole movement evolves inexorably as a single driven span, are its points of contact.

Like some other symphonies we have mentioned the *Symphonie Fantastique* has not the Classical time-scale, nor as a whole quite its sense of movement and tonal drama. The structure of the symphony reveals a loosening of the bonds between movements: the three middle movements are genre pieces instead of being deeply and functionally integral, a fact that must owe a great deal to the extraordinary composition of the work from odd numbers from the abandoned *Faust* ballet and the subsequently revived *Les Francs Juges*. On the other hand the *idée fixe*, providing external cyclic unification, becomes a dynamic and symbolic participant in the symphonic drama, as much a bearer of Furtwängler's thematic "destiny" (see page 25) as any thematic transformation of Beethoven's: what looks like loss and gain is evidently reinterpretation. The programme is sufficiently external, even incidental, to the music not to be a problem—in this respect the symphony is rather like Beethoven's *Pastoral*. The music goes its own way, in its own terms; only at the broadest level—for instance the relationship of the central movements to each other and to the rest—is it perhaps at all necessary to invoke any extramusical logic. We may wonder whether any of the arguments that have smouldered over this piece for being a "programme symphony" would have taken place if Berlioz had not provided a textual "explanation"; in his doing so we should understand, as Jacques Barzun has pointed out, that "by Berlioz's day, programme writing had become a custom ... in writing his Berlioz was obeying tradition: Lesueur, Knecht, Schubert, Spohr, Weber and Beethoven had preceded him".[29]

These remarks are generally true also of the programmatic significance of *Harold en Italie*. Here however there does appear a contradiction between the sonata form—evinced particularly by the first movement—and the still further general relaxation of the symphonic web. The first movement has in some ways a text-book orthodoxy, perhaps making Tom Wotton's point about Berlioz's "harmful" study of Beethoven, while the two middle movements carry so little structural weight that Einstein's description of them as "episodes" or "mere picturesque scenes" is scarcely an exaggeration, and the finale is frankly too ritornello-based to achieve much of the sonata drive it attempts. Like the *Symphonie Fantastique*, it makes some use of already existing music (originally composed for a cantata on the death of Mary, Queen of Scots, and the *Rob Roy* Overture).

In his *Roméo et Juliette* Berlioz grasps some of the implications of Beethoven's Ninth Symphony and expands the symphony both in the size of forces used (including the incorporation of vocal elements) and in duration (including extra movements). The work goes further along the path set by the earlier symphonies: it is still more of a *succession* of movements, and is associated yet further with programmaticism. This trait may be seen as the realization of another implication of Beethoven's—the tendency of the symphony to have extramusical significance. But there are fewer contradictions here than in *Harold*, because Berlioz now no longer allowed himself to be bound by the tighter exigencies of the traditional forms. The outcome is that there is much less of the traditional symphony here than in his previous works. That it does contain elements of the symphony it is important to stress, without necessarily subscribing to Berlioz's over-simplification that "it is neither an opera in concert form or a cantata, but a symphony with chorus". What it retains of the traditional form of the symphony is firstly the broad scheme and sequence of movements, mixed, and sometimes fused, with the vocal or other movements, and secondly (programme permitting) some of the internal formal operations of those movements. What it retains of the symphonic style is the fluidity and dynamism of symphonic development; the deeply relevant thematic integration, with its implicit concern for the fortunes and destinies of themes and motives; and the Beethovenian notion of conflict.

This last does not function at a highly interactive or dialectically meaningful level, but, in the general absence of important traditional means of organization and articulation, exists rather in the form of fairly static, contrasting blocks. Appropriately subtitled *Symphonie Dramatique*, the work looks towards Wagner—who was at the first performance in November 1839 in Paris, and who found it a "revelation of a new world of music". "Berlioz's secular scriptures", as Barzun has said, "composed and sung in the symphonic style, became Wagnerian opera as soon as music was reattached to acting and scenery: the Dramatic Symphony germinated the Music Drama".[30] As a "building of a world", it is a crucial link between Beethoven's Ninth and the symphonies of Mahler. And in its occasional blatant "story-telling"—where the music refers to, indeed needs, something outside itself—it anticipates Richard Strauss.

Two other works of Berlioz, with even more slender symphonic affiliations, deserve brief mention. *La Damnation de Faust* retreats still further from traditional symphonic thought, as implied by its subtitle *légende dramatique*. Yet at least one critic, in a somewhat tenuous claim, has found that "the symphonic spirit still persists in the rounded experience and the converging moral of each part".[31] And the *Symphonie Funébre et Triomphale*, though its internal forms may be irregular, traces at least a superficial symphonic "line" in the way it moves from the funeral march of the first movement to the apotheosis of the last.

Liszt, while apparently more removed than Berlioz from the Beethovenian symphony, was essentially closer to it. The confusion arises from the fact that Liszt's symphonic works are a more radical innovation-in-tradition—or reinterpretation—than those of Berlioz. His own approach to the symphonic problem was one of the most original of his century. It rested on the belief that Beethoven was dealing with metaphysical questions, and that the total form of his compositions was inseparable from the nature of the questions and the ways they were examined; this "explained" unorthodox form. His intuition arose from intimate knowledge of the Beethoven symphonies. Between 1837 and 1863 he transcribed all of them for the piano, a task undertaken partly out of his deep love for them, to make them more accessible and more popular. It is interesting to note that he had done the same for Berlioz's *Symphonie Fantastique* in 1833 and *Harold en Italie* in 1836. Like most men of his century involved with the sonata principle, Liszt regarded himself as belonging to the Beethovenian era. He followed Beethoven in using the sonata principle—now almost necessarily involving some notion of overt conflict—for philosophical ends: two obvious, if non-symphonic, works whose form is "explained" in this way are the C-sharp-minor quartet, Op. 131, and the B minor piano sonata.

Liszt came closest to articulating these points in his own words in a letter to Wilhelm von Lenz, an eminent Beethoven critic of the day, apropos of von Lenz's new book, *Beethoven et ses trois styles*.[32] The letter dates from 1852, well into the period of the composition of the symphonic poems:

Were it my place to categorize the different periods of the great master's thoughts, as manifested in his sonatas, symphonies, and quartets, I should certainly not fix the division into *three styles*, which is now pretty generally adopted and which you have followed; but, simply recording the questions which have been raised hitherto,

I should frankly weigh the *great* question which is the axis of criticism and of musical aestheticism at the point to which Beethoven had led us—namely, how far is tradition or recognized form a necessary determinant for the organism of thought?

The solution of this question, evolved from the works of Beethoven himself, would lead me to divide this work, not into three styles or periods—the words *style* and *period* being here only corollary subordinate terms, of a vague and equivocal meaning—but quite logically into two categories: the first, that in which tradition and recognized form contain and govern the thought of the master; and the second, that in which the thought stretches, breaks, recreates, and fashions the form and style according to its needs and inspirations.[33]

For our purposes, the only important thing to be said about the difference, in their philosophical aspect, between the symphonies of Beethoven and the symphonic poems of Liszt, is that Beethoven seldom gives any clue while Liszt, by appending programmes, often does—thus referring the listener directly to something outside the music (a text, a painting), where the ideas expressed inside it find a more explicit, and certainly a different, embodiment.

This is quite another thing from pictorialism in music; it is programme music only in the specious and not very helpful sense that a programme gives incidental accompaniment to the music and makes explicit what already exists with full independence and self-sufficiency (but in non-explicit musico-symbolic terms) in the piece. The relationship between music and programme is always tenuous in Liszt. Five of the first twelve symphonic poems do not have programmes at all. Those that do are not tyrannized by their programmes—there is a sense in which the music exists first and the programme second, or consequently. In the case of *Les Préludes* this is literally true: the work was written in 1848 as a prelude to *Les Quatre Elémens* (Op. 80), a work for male voice chorus and piano which was never published; and only much later, when Liszt decided to allow the prelude to stand as a separate piece, did he write a text to go with the music.

Les Préludes has its origin as an overture in common with many other symphonic poems. This says something important about the genesis of the new form. In it the experience of the single-movement dramatic overture, and of a century of symphonic writing, meet in a one-movement structure related to the quintessential sonata ideal, the traditional first movement. But the point now is the freedom that is exercised over this basic scheme: Gerald Abraham has found that seven of Liszt's symphonic poems can be discussed in terms of a *Bogen*.[34] The break, however, was not yet complete. In the two large symphonies as much as in the symphonic poems, Liszt took still further the tendency, inaugurated by Beethoven, to slow down harmonic progression; this, and the fact that his use of tonality, though generally unequivocal and still related to structure, was no longer structurally and dramatically *significant*, probably accounts for our feeling that these works have not the dynamic energy that we have come to recognize in the symphony.

Many other symphonic works of the second half of the nineteenth century similarly went through, and simultaneously belied, the conventional motions of key, since the means of integration and dramatic articulation was coming to depend on other factors. Theme was the most important of these: Liszt extended the cyclic techniques of Schubert and Schumann, and the *idée fixe* of Berlioz, into the idea of a synthesizing metamorphosis of themes, but one still capable of realizing a conflictual polarity. If his works are not ideal symphonically it is because the break was not clean, the new technique not yet perfect. The symphonic works are, finally, rather episodic.

In our discussion of Liszt we have avoided a too easy use of the term "programmatic". We have suggested that if the symphonic works are programmatic they can only be so either in the weak sense that some of them happen to be accompanied by texts, or else in the unusual sense that the Beethoven symphonies are "programmatic". Even in the case of the so-called programme symphonies of Berlioz we have found that the term has a very limited application.

Much of this goes against received musical notions, and it may be worth while to examine some of the underlying postulates a little more closely.

Insofar as we can, and do, speak about music as a "language" which has "meaning" for us, we are justified in saying that the *nature* of this meaning—here distinct from the meaning itself—differs from one piece to another. This difference is commonly, and crudely, expressed as the difference between the extremes of absolute music and programme music. We assume that the meaning of a piece of programme music is such that it can be paraphrased into common language. But if absolute music still "means" to us, what is the nature of this meaning? Or more to the point, why is this meaning not susceptible of expression in English? It is because this absolute music (a Bach fugue, a Mozart string quartet) uses a language of fluid sound symbols whose significance is "universal"—though this is not to deny that its genesis may have been particular and individual. But the meaning of these symbols is inexplicit, or better, non-specific.

In a work such as Beethoven's Fifth Symphony, however, a theme or motive can through a usage that defines its relationship to its context in a special way (though it still has no *a priori* meaning, or even a meaning outside this context) call to itself the specificity of a recognizable essence, or character. In such a case we may be tempted to call it a "protagonist", and may even want to give it an archetypal name—Death, Fate, Positive or Negative Force, etc. "Metaphors of darkness and light" said Dent, "abasement and exaltation, hesitancy and resolution we must allow to be legitimate, as hardly more than extensions of the notions of tension and relaxation which are fundamental to musical psychology".[35]

Beethoven's Sixth Symphony is for the most part such a work—and Beethoven articulated an important difference between this kind of symbolic language (which we will call "specific symbolization") and programmatic music in his insistence that despite the movement-headings—the *particular* genesis we spoke of earlier, here revealed—the music is still more an expression of feeling than painting.

Musical symbolization can become more inclusively specific than this—as in much of Nielsen, or even Wagner (consider especially *Tristan and Isolde*) where tonality also becomes specifically symbolic—without our needing to think that we have found a type of musical meaning whose nature is qualitatively different from Beethoven's.

What function have we left, then, for the term programmatic music? The only viable one has been hinted at earlier: we shall have to understand by it music that attempts to paint. Here the *symbol* will have been forsaken for the *image*. The crucial difference will be of one of two kinds. Either the meaning that will now inhere in the tonal language will not be a meaning that has flowered predominantly through musical context, but which it will have called to itself by *imitation* of the real, particular world; or the meaning will depend for its coherence on a programme, supplying the image to the music, tacked on from without. Finally, we must note that the simple existence or non-existence of a programme supplied by the composer has no *a priori* bearing on this distinction.

In the history of the symphony the specific symbolization type is almost exclusively a post-Beethoven phenomenon. Obvious examples, apart from the ones just mentioned, include Beethoven's Ninth Symphony, Schumann's Fourth Symphony, the *Symphonie Fantastique*, Liszt's symphonic poem *Hunnenschlacht*, and the *Faust* Symphony. Much of the mature music of Wagner—the furthest extension of the symphony in the nineteenth century along the line through Beethoven, Berlioz, and Liszt—belongs also to this type. In *Oper und Drama* Wagner was quite clear in regarding Beethoven as the instigator of this development; and his insistence on the primacy of a forming and shaping impulse reminds us of Liszt:

... a new, more subtly expressive type of instrumental melody ... [was] ... developed by Beethoven, yet a type not completely satisfactory in itself. "In the works of the second half of his artistic life," those in which the old, conventional formal moulds are broken by his profound emotion, "Beethoven is mostly unintelligible, or at any rate liable to be misunderstood, where he tries to convey some particular meaning with special clearness. He abandons the absolute-musical ... in order to speak in a language which, not being attached to a purely musical context, is only held together by a poetical idea that cannot be clearly expressed in the music itself."[36]

In the music dramas the "programme" is carried by the music itself in the form of verbal song. As the best programmes do, it gives precise, particular meaning to what is already inherent in the music as specific symbolization (this no longer dependent on subjects but on their logical extension, a leitmotiv network). And here is the importance of the text; for Wagner modern instrumental music, as invented by the later Beethoven,

"undeniably possesses a capacity for speech." Not precise speech; but we shall not now want it to be precise in itself; *the voice-part will give precision to the message* [my italics].[37]

Moreover,

instrumental music can also, through the power of association, recall past emotions and hence (as these vague emotions have been defined by the voice-part earlier in the drama) more precise thought-impressions. This, in fact, was the original function of the leitmotiv.[38]

The symphonic music of Richard Strauss is usually regarded as the furthest point to which story-telling in music had been taken. This view needs a great deal of qualification, but its general truth cannot easily be denied. It is Strauss, rather than Liszt, or Wagner, or even Berlioz, whom we may, in the light of the distinctions just made, sometimes be justified in speaking of as a programmatic symphonist. But we shall not understand Strauss unless we see that, far from this amounting to his symphonic excommunication, he was a fully conscious successor to Beethoven in the tradition that includes Berlioz, Liszt, and Wagner. He began, indeed, as a symphonic conservative, producing two "straight" symphonies in the early 1880's.

Broadly speaking, they are orthodox in form and "Leipzig" in idiom; and the second, in F minor, concludes with a recollection of earlier movements and a grand peroration. But Strauss soon began to feel that the only way to continue the Beethovenian tradition was to make certain changes in what he called the "musical-poetic content" and in the form—changes that were *already implied and to some degree realized in Beethoven*. In a single letter to von Bülow in August, 1888, he says almost precisely this. His arguments are basically the ones used by Wagner, Liszt, and by implication, Berlioz. The relevant passage is worth quoting at length:

A linking up with the Beethoven of "Coriolan", "Egmont", the "Leonore" III Overture, of "Les Adieux", above all with the late Beethoven, whose complete oeuvre, in my opinion, could never have been created without a poetic subject, seems to me the only course for the time being by which an *independent further* development of our instrumental music is yet possible. If I lack the artistic power and talent to achieve something worthwhile in this direction, then it is certainly better to let it rest with the big nine and their four distinguished offshoots ...

From the F minor symphony onwards I have found myself in a gradually ever increasing contradiction between the musical-poetic content that I want to convey and the ternary sonata form that has come down to us from the classical composers. In the case of Beethoven the musical-poetic content was for the most part completely covered by this very "Sonata form", which he raised to its highest point, wholly expressing in it what he felt and wanted to say. Yet already there are to be found works of his (the last movement of the A flat major sonata, Adagio of the A minor quartet, etc.), where for a new content he had to devise a new form. Now, what was for Beethoven a "form" absolutely in congruity with the highest, most glorious content, is now, after 60 years, used as a formula inseparable from our instrumental music (which I strongly dispute), simply to accommodate and enclose a "pure musical" (in the strictest and narrowest meaning of the word) content, or worse, to stuff and expand a content with which it does not correspond.

If you want to create a work of art that is unified in its mood and consistent in its structure, and if it is to give the listener a clear and definite impression, then what the author wants to say must have been just as clear and definite in his own mind. This is only possible through the inspiration by a poetical idea, whether or not it be introduced as a programme. I consider it a legitimate artistic method to create a correspondingly new form for every new subject, to shape which neatly and perfect is a very difficult task, but for that very reason the more attractive.[39]

Liszt had shown the way with the realization of the sonata principle in the symphonic poem. Apparently Strauss's highest ideal was no different from Liszt's: the programme should be a dispensable paraphrase, or objective co-relative, of the work's philosophical import already fully alive in the music in terms of a specific symbolization. "I am a musician first and last", he wrote when working on *Also Sprach Zarathustra*, "for whom all 'programmes' are merely the stimulus to the creation of new forms, and nothing more." And in July, 1905, he wrote to Romain Rolland:

> To me the poetic programme is no more than the basis of form and the origin of the purely musical development of my feelings—not, as you believe, a *musical description* of certain events of life. That would be quite contrary to the spirit of music ... To the listener, too, such an analytical programme should not be more than a pointer which can be used by those who so desire. Those who really understand how to listen to music probably don't need it at all ...[40]

Strauss was not always true to his ideal. In the best of the symphonic poems—say *Tod und Verklärung* or *Till Eulenspiegel*—the programme is incidental to the music. Here, as so often, it seems likely that Strauss published programmes because the public wanted them: as Ernst

Krause has pointed out, Strauss placed less importance on the publication of his programmes than did his public. But in deference to the shallow naturalism of his time Strauss began increasingly to write music that employed image rather than symbol. Works such as *Don Quixote* and the *Symphonia Domestica* are in our strict sense programmatic.

Strauss's reforms, however, seldom went so far that a traditional structure was not operative at some level, or that the principle of dualistic conflict was no longer basic to the work's dramatic articulation. *Macbeth* is a complex sonata form. It involves strong thematic opposites—one set of polarities symbolic of Macbeth and his wife (to use precise, i.e. textual, terms), and another of the conflict between love and war. The final version inverts traditional symphonic procedure by replacing the original D major with an ending in D *minor*. *Don Juan* is fundamentally a sonata-form movement carrying two large episodes within the development. It too traces a line of dramatic progress that is the inverse of the symphonic norm, moving from E major to E minor.

Tod und Verklärung articulates a conflict of two vast and violently opposed thematic complexes in terms of a fairly straightforward sonata structure that rises with superb judgement to an apotheosis in which the original tragic C minor is metamorphosed into a triumphant C major. The piece even retains dominant key relations between groups and a tonic recapitulation. *Till Eulenspiegel* is a rondo—a scherzo with "trios"—that also inverts the prototypical Beethovenian conclusion of triumph by ending with—in the precise terms of the text—a sentence of death for Till. *Zarathustra* ends tranquilly but without full resolution of its presiding conflict, an antagonism between keys on B and C—its symbols for the conflict between Man and Nature. The work is usually described as a free fantasia, but it is possible to discern in it, as Ian Spink has done,[41] a basic sonata structure. *Don Quixote* is in the form of symphonic variations, and has little to do with dualism. *Ein Heldenleben* involves a tremendous conflict (between symbols of the "hero" and his "adversaries") and a triumphant outcome. At one level its form is almost that of a fantasia; at another it is a vast sonata movement with scherzo and slow movement interpolated into the development, a recapitulation that coincides with the late stages of that development, and a coda.[42] The *Domestica* has some contact with the traditional four-movement structure of the symphony.

There remain a number of symphonists who do not fit immediately into either of the two great symphonic lines that run across the nineteenth century (and in the case of the second, have taken us already into the twentieth), but who may owe something to one or the other or both.

Bruckner is the most important of these, and his work stands with that of Brahms as the finest example of the renaissance of the Beethovenian symphony in the last third of the century. He differed from Brahms in having neither his acute "musicological" awareness of the past nor his distrust of the neo-Germans. The most powerful shaping influence on his symphonic style came from the late quartets and the symphonies of Beethoven, especially the Ninth, whose tremendous challenge Bruckner was the first composer fully to accept, and which was his most prevailing obsession. This was music he studied in detail, not objectively like Brahms, but from his own subjective premises. Other important influences came from Bach, Schubert (particularly the vocal works, but probably *not* the last two symphonies since, as Redlich has pointed out, it is unlikely that Bruckner came into contact with them), and Wagner. Though his symphonies differ from those of Beethoven in many obvious externals, and to a greater extent than do those of Brahms—the most unavoidable difference is their use of the Wagnerian time-scale— Bruckner's symphonies are "genuinely" Beethovenian in a number of essential ways. We may immediately indicate two of these, closely related to each other, and appropriate to this general discussion; others will become clear when we return to Bruckner shortly to mention some important details.

Firstly, Bruckner's symphonies reinvest the genre with an indestructible unity, a *Gestalt* in which each part has ultimately a bearing on every other part and a meaning only in the context of the whole, and in which the whole is greater than the sum of the parts. Secondly, they articulate a dialectic in which crucial dualities resting on a fluid, expansive syntax of theme *and key* reveal an absolute, indivisible identity with functions of structure and motion. A difference, but one which is less important than the points of contact, is that Bruckner's symphonies do not employ a technique of specific symbolization as do many Beethoven's, but rather one in which the symbols are more universal as in most pre- and many post-Beethoven symphonies. So much for his much-vaunted "Wagnerianism"—let along "programmaticism"! Another difference is that Bruckner's symphonies are not progressive temporal dramas in quite the way Beethoven's are. A symphony of Beethoven's is a journey in time, through time, as it were horizontally—an analogue of the experience of Becoming, dependent on growth through temporal conflict. A symphony of Bruckner's is outside of time, a search in which time has no place and for which we may wish to use the metaphors "inwards" or "downwards". This is probably what Robert Simpson means by describing the essence of Bruckner's music as "a patient search for pacification". He speaks of the music's tendency "to remove, one by one, disrupting or distracting elements, to seem to uncover at length a last stratum of calm contemplative thought". Consequently Bruckner's endings "are not really cumulative in the old sense; they are formal intensifications that blaze with calm."[43]

An inherited formal ground-plan—from the broad layout of the symphony to some of the minuter internal workings of the movements—is always discoverable in Bruckner, though in most respects far less easily than in Brahms: Bruckner tends to supersede sonata form, while Brahms still tries to use it. This leads for instance to a progressively greater integration of development and recapitulation, so that in the maturer symphonies sonata movements are frequently more aptly described (in Simpson's terms) as Statement, Expanded Counter-statement, and Coda. Among the more obvious results of the vast expansion the symphony undergoes in the hands of

Bruckner is the appearance of what looks like a third subject in the exposition—generically the old codetta theme
—and the great magnification of the micro-dualisms of
the Classical symphony, such as might operate between
consecutive or simultaneous lines within a single subject-
group. A good example of the magnification is the astonishing contrast, acknowledged and explained by Bruckner
himself, in the enharmonically written *Gesangsperiode* of
the finale of the Third Symphony, where a "polka" and a
"chorale" co-exist contrapuntally. Finally we must observe
that in addition to achieving a deep thematic unification, Bruckner, like Beethoven and others, also uses more
external means of integration: most of his symphonies
have some degree of cyclicism, and frequently a strong
structural as well as thematic resemblance between outer
movements.

Franck, though far less important, is perhaps in some
ways at least as anomalous as Bruckner. He represents a
highwater-mark of neo-German infatuation in France,
and he was in love with German polyphony; he was
overwhelmed by chromatic harmony and the modulatory
quicksands of the Wagnerian idiom and fired by Liszt's
technique of thematic metamorphosis, and he wrote a
consciously Beethovenian symphony by appropriating to
his style more or less orthodox procedures. Here was
another composer who believed himself to belong to the
Beethovenian tradition—even to be following the radical
formal precedents of Beethoven's late manner, though
there is little enough in the Symphony in D minor to suggest
this apart from the second movement's fusion of slow
movement and scherzo. As if these cross-currents are not
enough, the scherzo section of the second movement is
quite unambiguously Mendelssohnian in idiom. The
symphony is conventional in particulars of its key-plan, and
formally quite plainly so in two of its three movements;
even the hybrid movement resolves itself into a perfectly
simple ternary shape. It is a work of intricate cyclicism and
is shot through with thematic transformations. It partakes
convincingly in the Beethovenian ethic of conflict.

Many of Franck's followers shared his dispositions—for

instance Chausson, whose B flat Symphony is cyclical and Beethovenian in the manner of its thematic growth and purpose, and d'Indy, who described his huge Symphony in B flat as a (Beethoven) conflict between good and evil. Saint-Saëns's Third Symphony is another good example of the late French Romantic mixing of Lisztian techniques, a basically conventional outline, and a dramatic growth that yields an apotheosis out of the conflict, but it is not typical of the composer's other, more Classical strain, which later found a culmination in the neo-Classicism of the Symphony in C by Dukas.

Like his older compatriot Smetana, Dvořák came early under a powerful neo-German influence. But above all he revered Beethoven and Schubert; and his career as a symphonist may be seen as a struggle to find his way through these sympathies—as well as others, such as his nationalistic proclivity to use folk idioms, and his later Brahmsian inclinations—and to write the great Beethovenian symphony which he felt it his duty to do. The interest in Beethoven is clear from the start: Dvořák's First Symphony is in C minor and its four movements use the same key-scheme as the movements of Beethoven's C minor Symphony. The two symphonies that follow it suffer from contradictions between an idiom owing much to Liszt and Wagner and some of the conventional forms onto which the music is simply pegged; as in the First, there are problems of unity and indeed of the very fundamental application of the sonata principle. A rejection of the neo-German influence is incipient in the Fourth Symphony, and complete in the Fifth where now the Classical models are paramount—as filtered through the multiple lenses of the Mendelssohn and Schumann symphonies, the *Pastoral*, and Schubert. Yet even here sonata form is followed rather than dynamically used; delightful this Fifth Symphony may be, but there is little single-mindedness about it and insufficient thrust. These remarks are less true of the finale, the weightiest movement and one that has a genuine dramatic urge. It looks in the direction of the graver Beethoven, proposing a conflict and finding an ultimate triumph. In this sense the movement stands outside the orbit of the other three movements—perhaps the consequence of an unsuccessful application of the *Pastoral* precedent of a late exposition of conflict.

In the last three symphonies—the Seventh, Eighth, and Ninth—Dvořák brought the problems that beset the earlier symphonies as close to full solution as he was able. Particularly in the Seventh, written under the inspiration of Brahms's Third which he had recently heard, and in the Ninth, is Dvořák's virtual mastery of the Classical symphonic techniques and principles evident. And the approach is individual: for instance in a major ending to a minor-key symphony (i.e. the Ninth) the temptation, so universal at this time, to write a triumphant peroration in naive imitation of Beethoven, is resisted—and properly so, for Dvořák's contrasts are less a matter of conflict than of Classical dualistic imbalance. In the Ninth Symphony, too, Dvořák brought the cyclic technique that he had used so often in his symphonies to a state of high intricacy: indeed in the development of the finale it ceases to be a mere binding device and becomes integral to the symphonic denouement, revealing connections between the first subjects of the first three movements, and between these and the material of the last movement. Like Haydn, Dvořák developed a rare ability to harness folk music—or at any rate its idiom—to symphonic ends; like Schubert, with whom he had a profound natural affinity, he learnt at length to come to terms with Beethoven, to distil and concentrate his own great inventiveness, and to master the Classical symphonic style. His best symphonic work is associated with—indeed helped to bring about—the rebirth of the symphony in the late nineteenth century.

There is authority, and at least some justice, in Dvořák's remark to James Huneker that Tchaikovsky was really a composer of suites. If Dvořák was thinking of Tchaikovsky's first three symphonies in particular and of his notorious "seams" in general, the remark has at any rate more justice than Bruckner's frequent description of the symphonies of Schumann as *Sinfonietten*. But we should not think that Tchaikovsky was a mindless joiner of tunes or that he was any less aware of the symphonic heritage than other symphonic composers of his generation. His struggle for formal mastery is too often spoken of to bear repetition in full: "Sometimes one must do oneself violence", he wrote to Nadejda von Meck in June, 1878,

> must sternly and pitilessly take part against oneself . . . I have always suffered from my want of skill in the management of form. Only after strenuous labour have I at last succeeded in making the form of my compositions correspond, more or less, with their contents.[44]

And inevitably we find that when Tchaikovsky is thinking of a model he is thinking of Beethoven; like nearly every other symphonist of his century, Tchaikovsky believed he belonged to the Beethovenian tradition and that in his own way he was helping to perpetuate it. In a letter to Taneiev in March, 1878, he wrote:

> With all that you say as to my [Fourth] Symphony having a programme, I am quite in agreement. But I do not see why this should be a mistake. I am far more afraid of the contrary; I do not wish any symphonic work to emanate from me which has nothing to express, and consists merely of harmonies and a purposeless design of rhythms and modulations. Of course, my symphony is programme music, but it would be impossible to give the programme in words; it would appear ludicrous and only raise a smile ... I must tell you that in my simplicity I imagined the plan of my symphony to be so obvious that everyone would understand its meaning, or at least its leading ideas, without any definite programme ... Throughout the work I have made no effort to express any new thought. In reality my work is a reflection of Beethoven's Fifth Symphony; I have not copied his musical contents, only borrowed the central idea. What kind of programme has his Fifth Symphony, do you think?

How one answers Tchaikovsky's question may depend on what one understands by programme. But Tchaikovsky has already partially qualified the term; and we should in reply suggest that it may be more useful to employ the coinage

"specific symbolization" here than to speak of a programme. As for his own programme, the explanatory
text he sent to von Meck was written *post factum*, and he
indicated that he was by no means satisfied with it—or even
sure of the possibility of writing an "explanation". Some of
the other numbered symphonies have suggestive titles in
the manner of Beethoven's *Pastoral*, but the Sixth—of all
Tchaikovsky's symphonies the most consistently specific in
its symbolization—gives away no verbal clue (unless it be
between bars 201 and 205 in the first movement, where the
brass play a passage from the Orthodox Requiem associated
with "resting with the saints"). "Its programme will remain
an enigma for everyone", said the composer. "Let them
guess ...". One may wonder how often Beethoven uttered
the same comment over *his* symphonies! But Tchaikovsky
did not turn to Beethoven only for justification of his so-
called programmaticism. With perhaps rather less good
cause, but with no less enthusiasm not to be excluded from
the Beethoven tradition, Tchaikovsky in the same letter
quoted above replied to Taneiev's charge that the flaw of
his Fourth Symphony was its incorporation of "phrases
which sound like ballet music":

> In that case how can you reconcile yourself to the
> majority of Beethoven's symphonies, for in them you will
> find similar melodies on every page? ... I do not see why
> dance tunes should not be employed episodically in a
> symphony, even with the avowed intention of giving a
> touch of coarse, everyday humour. Again I appeal to
> Beethoven, who frequently had recourse to similar
> effects.[46]

One of the great difficulties Tchaikovsky had to face as a
symphonist was his natural love of intransigent, self-
contained melodic types. Russian folk-song is one of these—
and it need not be authentic folk-song, for its idiom alone
may be equally unsymphonic. Tchaikovsky was highly
proficient at writing in this idiom: "I grew up in the
backwoods", he wrote to Mme. von Meck, "saturating
myself from earliest childhood with the inexplicable beauty
of the characteristic traits of Russian folk-song". The

Second Symphony is built to a large degree on folk-song or its idiom (hence the later nickname of *Little Russian*). The other most common "problem" type is the self-sufficient Romantic *cantilena*, which insofar as it has some place in the work of most symphonies of the nineteenth century from Schubert onward, and inevitably militates against the Classical syntax of "developing variation", is one of the century's most familiar symphonic difficulties. But we have seen that these composers ultimately found their own solutions—more, or less, satisfactory according to the genius of the composer—and as we shall see Tchaikovsky was to do likewise. Inseparable from the problem of melody was another of Tchaikovsky's great problems: the tendency, in the absence of material capable of creating and sustaining a subtle and dynamic dialectical structure, to *impose* shape on the material by simply forcing it into orthodox formal patterns. Hence most of Tchaikovsky's sonata movements may be seen to depend on a formal stereotype rather than to create their own unique, unrepeatable internal relations. Hence also the frequent episodic nature of some of his symphonies, the merely contingent relationships between some of their movements, the contradictions between the conventional key manouevres and Tchaikovsky's more "natural" proclivity for the side-stepping modulations that undermine purposeful tonality, and the frequent irrelevance—in the absence of the necessary tension of a latent unity—of what are posed *by the form* as contrasts of a "dualistic" nature.

The Fourth Symphony is a prodigous step forward in Tchaikovsky's symphonic career. The symphony is integrated to an amazing degree; it is organized in terms of a single *Gestalt*—represented by the opening horn theme—on the basis of which it is possible to account rationally for every important move in the work, as Alan Walker has done,[47] even to the point of explaining the unusual key arrangements. Its highly dramatic nature depends on the violence of its thematic contrasts which, even if they don't *engage* in conflict in the usual way, sufficiently acknowledge each other by virtue of their underlying unity that their mere juxtaposition generates much of the crisis. The forms, though still unmistakably related to the orthodox types, are now unusual, and depend on the exigencies of the material and the composer's musico-dramatic purpose. When folk-song is used, as in the last movement, it is with a careful eye to its possibilities, and its use is appropriate to its particular position in the symphony. But the Fifth Symphony, from a strictly symphonic point of view, is a regression. Packed with lyrical, intractable "tunes"—rather than subjects—which are moreover too self-centred for any dualistic engagement, the work falls into the errors of formalism and attempts a pseudo-symphonicism that cannot disguise its fundamentally balletic disposition. The last movement, however, redeems something for the work by finding a more symphonic sense of direction and a truly dynamic motion. The Sixth Symphony copes with Tchaikovsky's perennial problems in a masterly way. The richly lyrical element in the work, since it cannot be banished, is rendered symphonically viable by being vested with a high dramatic purpose as a persistent polarity in the work, and by its deep and revealing thematic integration. It is confined, moreover, to areas where it is fairly easily dealt with (such as the second-subject stage of the first move-ment), and is closely associated with material that *is* dynamic and developmental (such as the first movement's first subject). In this first movement the polarization spoken of above is clearly evident; and it appears in association with the keys of B minor and D major. The way these theme-key-mood complexes transmute themselves into the various movements while usually retaining their identity and their key-centres of B and D accounts for the symphony's specific symbolization mentioned earlier. This symphony—with the Fourth—gives some support to Hans Keller's view that "Tchaikovsky's individual contribution to the development of symphonic thought was the discovery and integration of new and violent contrasts ..."[48] Most of Tchaikovsky's symphonies use the cyclic technique to some extent. His symphonic poems belong largely to the autonomous, pre-Straussian type, in that they are not conditioned by their programmes and so are in a sense independent of them.

Most are explicable in terms of sonata structures—some of these, as in the symphonies, relating to the formal stereotype, others expanded and varied by interpolations.

In Tchaikovsky's compatriots, Borodin and Balakirev, we encounter a phenomenon surprising in nineteenth-century symphonic terms: symphonists who did not feel the weight of the symphonic heritage or experience the need to come to terms with Beethoven. With a less European consciousness than Tchaikovsky's, these Russians wrote, it is true to say, without a past, out of nothing. In this sense they are on the outer fringe of symphonic practice in the nineteenth century; but we can see now that this was part of their strength, and it helped them to make some refreshing and original symphonic contributions. Their approach to the time-honoured concept of dualism is a case in point. In general they preserve just enough of the appearance of dualism to show that they know about it, and then proceed to prove that for them it doesn't exist in any meaningful sense at all.[49] Borodin's First Symphony has a first movement that begins by looking like sonata form but ends by destroying the illusion of duality as the subjects are shown really to be one and the same. In the first movement of the Second Symphony, the second subject, chameleon-like, soon takes on the appearance of the first; at the same place in the Third Symphony, the second group clarifies rather than polarizes the first. Balakirev's First Symphony has a monothematic first movement and appropriate Lisztian metamorphosis—Liszt was of course a powerful influence in Russia at this time—in order to give a (non-dualistic) second-subject "shape" and to supply the principle by which the music can be said to progress; typically for a Russian symphony, it shuns orthodox developmental technique, but it also goes a stage further in denying all sectionality and forfeiting "block" recapitulation for spasmodic recollections in passing. Also unusual in these symphonies are the key-changes, often favouring such unorthodox relationships as those between tonalities semitonally adjacent (as in the first movement of Balakirev's Second Symphony, where the first subject is in D minor and the second in D flat major). Associated with this

is the frequent use of modulation for purposes of colour
and variation rather than strictly as a means of articulating structure. With the displacement of the old syntax by
one based more on folk-song, and the corresponding
weakening of harmony as a function of movement and
direction, rhythm takes on new importance as the most
vital means of conveying motion. What is common to all
these changes is the most radical loosening the symphony
had yet seen of its logical Teutonic method, represented
principally by its highly developed dialectical technique.
The wheel had come full circle. Borodin and Balakirev
raised once again the question whether the symphony could
retain any meaningful relationship with its past, or whether
it had—as they seem inadvertently to suggest—to learn to
forget and set out in a new direction. This question already
leads us into the chapters that follow; but first we must
review with a little closer attention to detail some of the
more observable and specific changes in the life of the
symphony up to this time.

IV

We turn first to the opening movement. As we have seen,
Haydn refined the initial adagio of the church sonata into a
prefix to the first movement, and it is common to find a
slow introduction in his symphonies after the early 1770's.
Gradually he made its relationship with the ensuing allegro
more complex and more necessary by means of subtle
thematic integration. Later the introduction might contain
seeds of the allegro or even, as in No. 98, its principal
theme; sometimes it might instead have seeds of the slow
movement (as in Nos. 86 and 92). Occasionally (for instance
No. 103) the introduction made a dramatic return during
the course of the first movement. Particularly in the
"Salomon" symphonies there was also now a metrical
similarity between the introduction and the allegro, though
the principle of contrast—involving for instance a minor-
mode introduction for a major allegro—was retained.
Haydn's earliest second groups appear in the dominant

minor or largely avoid a *thematic* contrast; No. 41 of the *Sturm und Drang* period is one of the first to have a second group that contrasts with the first in every possible way. In the later symphonies—after 1785—the groups are either thematically identical, or closely related (in both these cases for the sake of unity), or else quite distinct. Thematic identity, of course, does not mean lack of dualism so long as there is *tonal* opposition. Haydn wrote scarcely any real developments before the mid-1760's; then, in the *Sturm und Drang*, he began to find a working-out technique based mainly—but not always—on the given material. He perfected the technique with the "new manner" of the 1780's, but it was his later Symphony No. 102 that especially heightened the contrapuntal drama of the development with the idea of thematic *conflict* and caused the re-capitulation to enter, in Robbins Landon's words, "as the dazzling conqueror of a titanic thematic battle". After the meeting with Mozart in 1781, Haydn added weight to his codas by giving them a developmental importance (e.g. No. 100). The gain from that meeting—and from each composer's growing acquaintance with the other's music—was reciprocal: in 1783 Mozart wrote his first slow introduction, to the *Linz* Symphony. And in some of Mozart's late symphonies the striking, even overt, thematic relationship between contrasting groups suggests that Mozart was wanting to assimilate the contrasts to each other at a thematic level under the influence of Haydn's frequent monothematicism. Mozart also learnt a good deal from Haydn's developments. Of course, the mutual spiritual gains were far greater than any of these.

Beethoven used the slow introduction in his First, Second, Fourth, and Seventh Symphonies—and with characteristic individuality: in the First Symphony it begins in the "wrong" keys, and in the Seventh it seems to outline the ensuing sonata drama in analogous tonal and thematic terms. His many formal innovations, such as the choice of B flat major for the second group in the Ninth Symphony, and the introduction of a new theme in the development of the *Eroica*, are well known; less clearly understood are his radical and far-reaching changes in the operation of the dualistic principle in the *Eroica* and in the Seventh Symphony, which we shall only mention here but will need to examine at a later, more appropriate stage. With the development section as the decisive, central stage in the thematic and tonal struggle of the movement, the recapitulation often follows closely and with great dramatic impact upon its climax, as the issue of that conflict, or the "victor", or the tremendous reassertion of Beethoven's own will. Beethoven's codas, like many of Haydn's, are often developmentally extended, but with this difference, that they may now bring the movement to its highest, most dramatic climax.

In Schubert the more consistently overt thematic connection between the slow introduction and its sequel is an aspect of the external unification that we have seen become increasingly necessary from the time of Beethoven onwards. Of his symphonies, all but the Fifth and the Eighth have introductions; in most of these (i.e. the First, Third, Fourth, and Ninth) the principal subject of the movement is anticipated in some form in the introduction. Moreover, the introduction may be recalled later in the movement (as in the First and Ninth Symphonies); and it may be less slow than formerly (in the Ninth it is andante). Schubert's subjects are unusual in their dangerous tendency to be disparate and lyrically self-absorbed; and some of his second groups are tonally unorthodox. Developments are invariably unconventional. They may be virtual non-developments, as in the Fourth Symphony, where little happens other than the repetition of the first subject outside the main keys of the exposition; or they may be superb reinterpretations of the Classical ideal, as in the last two symphonies, where the shape and identity of the subjects is retained, despite sustained conflict, by means of a technique that places them in changing contexts and surrounds them with cellular working of a more orthodox developmental kind. Recapitulations often evade the tonal and dramatic implications of sonata by returning the groups in related keys instead of in the tonic, and by their sometimes formalistic similarity to the exposition.

In the *Scotch* Symphony Mendelssohn also secures an overt

thematic connection between the slow introduction (again an andante, this time *con moto*) and the allegro; the two sections are drawn still closer together by the partial return of the introduction as a kind of second coda to the movement. But this introduction departs further from the Classical model in being fully melodic and periodic rather than a motivic flux. Similarly, the *Reformation* Symphony uses the Dresden Amen in the introduction. The *Scotch* also ignores the normal Classical community of metre between the introduction and the allegro: here the one is in 3/4, the other in 6/8. Another departure in the way of diversity is the change from *Allegro un poco agitato* to *Assai animando* for the second group, a diversification countered to some extent by the clear motivic binding of the two groups. In the *Italian* Symphony the real dualistic charge lies elsewhere than between the traditional groups, but as with the comparable case of the *Eroica* a full explanation of this must await a more appropriate stage of our study. Significantly, the movement is also like the first movement of the *Eroica* in that the development introduces a new subject. The development typically abounds in Classical techniques; it also has a genuine thematic struggle, which is taken up again in the coda.

Only the Third of Schumann's symphonies has no slow introduction. All contain important thematic premonitions of the ensuing allegro; the Second and Fourth in addition have material that appears elsewhere in the symphony. The introduction of the First Symphony is "andante un poco sostenuto", and it returns at the beginning of the recapitulation. On Beethoven's precedent Schumann sometimes introduced—or recapitulated—a group in a "wrong" key at first, only finding the "right" key later on. In any case he was capable of choosing an unusual key area for a thematic group, such as G minor (instead of the orthodox B flat major) for the exposition of the second group in the *Rhenish* and the analogous C minor for its recapitulation. In the highly unified Fourth Symphony there is no new material associated with the second-subject stage—only a change of key, as in many Haydn symphonies. Schumann's developments are less Classically competent than Mendelssohn's; and some lack the unifying thrust of a single urge impelling the development toward the recapitulation. New material in the development is not uncommon—the Fourth Symphony, for example, has a new *pair* of themes, which engage in combat. The same symphony has a partly suppressed recapitulation, which, however, deploys the second development theme at the second-subject stage. The First Symphony, apart from having a new theme in the development, diversifies still further in the coda, which is quicker, and introduces yet another theme.

Brahms used a slow introduction in the opening movement only once in his symphonies—in the First—and there it provides germinal anticipations of the ensuing allegro, and is recalled in the coda. His second groups are powerful contrasts, and nowhere more so than in the Third Symphony, where the group enters in the unorthodox mediant (A major), brings with it a metrical change (from 6/4 to 9/4), and is reinforced by an unambiguous change of instrumental colour (mainly woodwind based, as against a mainly string-based first group). In the Fourth Symphony the first group, in E minor, is followed by a second group placed unusually in the dominant minor; but the exposition ends in B major. Brahms's developments— thoroughly integral; dynamic, single spans motivically worked; dramatic and climactic—are among the most remarkable reincarnations ever of the Beethoven-style development. His recapitulations can also be dramatic in the Beethoven manner. His codas tend to be unlike those of Beethoven in their brevity and their avoidance of development.

Berlioz used the slow introduction *qua* slow introduction in two of his symphonies: the *Symphonie Fantastique* and *Harold en Italie*. Both follow the old precedent of anticipating a major-mode allegro by a minor-mode introduction. Both are unusually long and to a degree periodic rather than motivic. In the *Symphonie Fantastique* premonitions of the *idée fixe* are deeply embedded into the texture of the introduction and germinal to it. In *Harold* the *idée fixe* is proposed more openly; and the section begins to sound rather more like a slow movement than an introduction. The adagio (in 3) and the allegro (in 6/8) are perhaps more separate, and, despite the obvious thematic connections, more merely incidental to each other, than ever before in the symphony. In the *Symphonie Fantastique* the real development does not take place in the brief section between exposition and recapitulation but is saved for the long and climactic coda. It is an aspect of this fluid, evolutionary movement that the recapitulation arrives virtually unnoticed—and initially in the dominant, attaining the tonic only *after* the onset of the second subject. *Harold*, by contrast, is a rigid, orthodox structure, scarcely mollified by the reverse recapitulation. But it has a genuine and compelling development. The coda, as in the earlier work, is Beethovenian in its length and developmental nature.

Formal norms are often disguised, reinterpreted, or simply abandoned in the symphonic works of Liszt and his successors—as they were to a large extent already in the later symphonic writings of Berlioz. But more often they are still recognizable. Both the *Faust* Symphony and *Les Préludes*, to take two typical examples from Liszt, have slow introductions; both have anticipations of first-subject material. The "free" sonata of the *Faust* Symphony poses a conflict between multiple themes, or complex subject-groups, defined roughly by their opposing tendencies, one striving towards "light", the other towards "darkness". *Les Préludes* is in this respect more regular: apart from the new, slower time-scale which is not our concern here, there is hardly anything more unusual about the subjects than the choice of the mediant major instead of the dominant for the second group. The development section of *Les Préludes* may be described as extrapolatory and derivative rather than toughly analytic in the Classical manner, and it has a big quasi-slow movement (*Allegretto pastorale*) interpolation. There is a tonic recapitulation with the groups returning in reverse order. The *Faust* Symphony follows a brief, incremental development with a brief reprise. In Strauss the problems of recognition become greater—though not in a work such as *Tod und Verklärung*, with its large introduction pregnant with thematic germs of what is to come, its *meno mosso* second group in the dominant,[50] its vast conflictual development in which old material is made the basis of proliferation and extrapolation, and its succinct tonic-*major* recapitulation extending into a coda whose apotheosis insists—on behalf of the whole piece—on its direct succession to the Beethoven heritage.

With the notable exception of the Fifth Symphony, Bruckner did not use the slow introduction. The typical hushed stillness, the motionlessness, of his openings suggest that he took instead the beginning of Beethoven's Ninth for his symphonic model. The Fifth Symphony, however, opens with an adagio introduction that is full of thematic cells and motives pertaining to the whole work; and they anticipate later conflicts in the way they stand to each other in relationships of tense thematic and tonal contrast. The introduction returns at its original speed during the development.

Dika Newlin has keenly observed that Bruckner's principal subjects can nearly always be seen as a synthesis of the Wagnerian *melos* and the 'particle construction' of the Classical symphony. She cites as further proof of this their "classic symphonic urgency which is symbolized by dotted rhythms or martial I-V-I fanfares".[51]

Bruckner's second groups are sometimes in a slower tempo; and when they are tonally unorthodox they are usually (e.g. in the Fourth and Eighth Symphonies) followed by a sequel that ends the exposition in an orthodox key. Bruckner's so-called third subjects proportionally take up no more of the exposition than did Classical codetta themes from which they are generically derived, and they are normally related to previous material. His developments, while of course on a greatly expanded time-scale, are still no less real for that. They support and are generated by a tonal drama as fully and functionally modulatory as any Classical development. The recapitulations, insofar as they are recognizable as such, usually return the first group in the tonic, but especially in the later symphonies—and partly owing to their developmental and recapitulatory syntheses—the other groups tend to appear in related keys.

The codas seem long only in relation to music on a different time-scale. They are, like Beethoven's, the dramatic outcome of the movement—for instance, tragic in the Eighth Symphony, in the Seventh a blaze of E major light with the first subject resolved back into its tensionless common-chordal origins.

The remaining composers can be passed over quickly, as they offer little that we have not already seen. Dvořák's introductions, when they appear, are not always slow and sometimes contain a motto that returns during the movement and perhaps again later in the symphony; that in the Ninth Symphony is more conventional, being aperiodic on the Classical precedent and foreshadowing the cyclic first subject of the movement. If the earlier developments tend to be psuedo-Classical, by the time of the Ninth Symphony Dvořák had brought a host of Classical developmental techniques under his pen; the Ninth also has a developing coda. All Tchaikovsky's symphonies except the First begin with a slow passage that usually returns later in the movement, and may appear literally or in meta-morphosis in other movements as well. Sometimes, as in the Sixth Symphony, it is germinal to the thematic material of the symphony as a whole. Tchaikovsky's finest developments are satisfactory compromises with Classical techniques: in the Fourth Symphony he surrounds the first subject with dynamic contrapuntal elements, finds new and often dramatic settings for it, and varies it; in the Sixth he fully extends the first subject in the exposition and gleans from its organic proliferations much material that is developmentally susceptible; he also makes good use of transformation in this symphony. His best recapitulations—belonging to these same two works—are, like many of Beethoven's, precipitated by the climax of the development and carried by its gathered momentum. Some of his codas introduce old material in new-sounding transformations.

We turn next to the middle movements. Haydn's slow movements deepen from the early binary-ternary hybrid andantes into adagios, often in an elementary sonata form. Variations—of differing types and in different hybrid combinations—are the most popular form of the later slow movements. Haydn's truly symphonic minuets—those which have forsaken their courtly inhibitions—belong to the symphonies after 1785: indeed in No. 86 Robbins Landon has discovered "a miniature movement in sonata form". Their trios are sometimes overtly thematically related, sometimes contrasting. Mozart's slow movements follow a similar course of deepening into broad adagios; the early symphonies (before the great triad of 1773) characteristically have andantes, sometimes in the dominant, while the andantes in some of the last symphonies are usually profound movements bearing little relationship to the earlier type. Sonata form is not uncommon among the mature slow movements. Mozart's last minuets are allegrettos, fully symphonicized movements capable of exploiting the possibilities of contrast between minuet and trio to intensely dramatic ends—as in the G minor Symphony. Occasionally Mozart wrote two independent trios.

Beethoven's slow movements tend to be adagios or andantes—with the allegretto "march" movement of the Seventh Symphony and the "allegretto scherzando" of the Eighth as the two notable exceptions. Sonata, rondo, and variation, are among the forms used. In the Second Symphony the slow movement is situated in the unusual key of the dominant. The title "scherzo" is used in only two of the symphonies, but it is appropriate to all—including the First, with its *allegro molto e vivace* indication. Remarkable among the scherzos are those in the Fourth, Sixth, Seventh, and Ninth Symphonies, whose trios call for a change of tempo, thus moving the movement away from the more homogeneous Classical type; in two of these symphonies, moreover, the Fourth and the Seventh, there are two identical trios. The scherzo in the Ninth is one of the first ever to be placed second in a four-movement symphony, and also one of the first to use sonata form for its scherzo section—and is still more unusual for having the second subject of this sonata form in the key of the flattened leading-note. Schubert's slow movements are basically more simply shaped than Beethoven's—nearly all are ternary structures. Before his Sixth Symphony Schubert used the word minuet rather than scherzo, though the generally rapid tempi and frequent syncopation of these movements suggest that they are already moving towards the scherzo ideal. The Ninth Symphony's scherzo is in sonata form, and has a new theme in its development.

Mendelssohn's *Italian* Symphony has an andante "march" movement in the manner of the second movement of Beethoven's Seventh Symphony; the scherzo has a trio unusually situated in the dominant. The scherzo of the *Scotch* Symphony is unconventional on four counts: it appears as the second movement, it is in simple duple time instead of triple, it is a sonata movement, and it has no trio. Schumann wrote two successive slow movements into his *Rhenish* symphony, neither of them in itself very traditional: the first is a brief intermezzo, the other a majestic neo-Baroque polyphonic movement. His other slow movements—with the exception of the *adagio espressivo* of the Second Symphony—are also genre pieces: a larghetto and a *Romanze*, the latter in the dominant minor. His scherzos are still more eccentric. The First and Second Symphonies have two dissimilar trios; in the former, one trio is in a quicker tempo, and in the latter the scherzo is in 2/4. The Third Symphony, like the Second, has the scherzo as the second movement; and it is an original synthesis of orthodox scherzo-and-trio form and sonata form, in which there is no recapitulation of the second subject. Though marked "scherzo", it is moderato in tempo and really more like a *Ländler*. The Fourth Symphony, like two of Beethoven's, has two identical trios. In Brahms, too, adagio is the atypical marking for the slow movement: three out of the four in the symphonies are andantes. The scherzos slow down to allegrettos. None is unequivocally in scherzo-and-trio form—least of all in the Second Symphony, where the movement is a theme and variations, and in the Fourth, where the movement is a sonata structure. In the First and Fourth Symphonies, moreover, the movement is in 2/4.

With Berlioz the genre piece still more invades the centre of the symphony, sometimes, as we have seen, bringing with it an exclusiveness that undermines unity; sometimes, too, the character of the genre overrides the inherited character of slow movement or scherzo. Thus the allegretto march in *Harold* is less of a symphonic movement than is the second part of Beethoven's Seventh Symphony, which is its precedent, and the serenade in the same work is hardly a scherzo, though the flanking sections of its ternary structure are certainly scherzo-like. (The movement can of course be seen as a free reinterpretation of the scherzo-and-trio idea, though in inverse formal proportions). The *Symphonie Fantastique* has *two* unusual "scherzo" movements: the *Valse* (on the analogy of the symphonic use of the minuet and the *Ländler*) which falls second, and the penultimate *Marche au supplice*, in sonata form.

In the symphonic works of Liszt and Strauss, as we have already suggested, slow movements and scherzos generally exist, if at all, in the form of radical reinterpretations which preserve something of their principle but usually little of their outward shape or definition. It is in the symphonies of Bruckner that the great Classical and Beethoven-type slow movements and scherzos come once again to life. Not for half a century had there been adagios of such breadth and profundity as are found here. Though vast, these movements are nearly always basically ternary strctures; the adagio of the Sixth Symphony, in sonata form, is the notable exception. Sometimes they bear an extraordinary tonal relationship to the principal key of the symphony: the slow movements of the minor-key Third and Eighth Symphonies are in the key of the flat supertonic major, and that of the D minor Ninth is in the (natural) supertonic major. Though Bruckner usually calls his scherzos explicitly by that name, they commonly owe a good deal to the Schubertian *Ländler*—and their trios may do so as well. The exclusively scherzo sections of these movements are characteristically in a concentrated sonata form. One scherzo and three trios are in duple time, and most of the trios, and very occasionally even the second subject of the sonata-scherzo, prescribe a new tempo. In the Eighth and Ninth Symphonies the scherzo is placed second.

Franck's merging of the central movements in his D minor Symphony takes the form of an allegretto ternary movement in B flat minor in which the central G minor section is scherzo-like and even has its own "trio" in the flat submediant major. The repeat of the "scherzo" merges and then fuses with the reprise of the first section to complete what is a highly original movement. Dvořák's slow movements are andantes or adagios, usually in ternary form; his scherzos are characteristically furiants, though he was also capable of writing a slower and more graceful Brahmsian intermezzo-type movement—such as the wistful *allegretto grazioso* of the Eighth Symphony. Tchaikovsky's slow movements show us nothing new until the Sixth Symphony, which takes the unprecedented step of having a full-scale adagio as the finale. His scherzos owe something to Berlioz—particularly with regard to the symphonic treatment of the waltz (in the third movement of the Fifth Symphony and the 5/4 "waltz" movement of the Sixth). His symphonic assimilations of the march are perhaps also more indebted to Berlioz than to other composers who had similarly incorporated it (consider especially the third movement of the Sixth Symphony and the trio in the scherzo of the Fourth). And indeed the very use of two "scherzos" in the last symphony, as in the Third, is a structural idiosyncrasy which has a precedent in Berlioz. In the matter of key-schemes Tchaikovsky was much more orthodox than Borodin and Balakirev; for instance, the slow movement of Borodin's First Symphony is in D, while the principal key is E flat, and the corresponding movement in Balakirev's First Symphony is in D flat, while the main key is C; and the scherzo of Borodin's Second Symphony is in F, a tritone removed from the principal key of B. Also worth noting is that the slow movement of Balakirev's First Symphony is, unusually, a sonata-rondo, still more irregular for having its second subject in the key of the augmented second; his Second Symphony has a slow movement called "Romanza", after the early Romantic type. The scherzo of Balakirev's First Symphony falls second. The same movement in his next symphony has its scherzo section in a sonata form which, during the reprise after the trio, replaces the old second subject with the trio theme.

In the last part of this more detailed, but necessarily brief, survey, we must examine the history of the finale. Quite early in Haydn's symphonic career he began to take special care of the finale; even before the *Sturm und Drang* he gave it a new dramatic emphasis. His early finales were ternary or rondo affairs, but from about the time of his meeting with Mozart he started to add an intellectual strength to the movement by crossing rondo with sonata; thus came into being what we know as the sonata-rondo. Thereafter Haydn used sonata and rondo separately, as well as in their new hybrid combination, to shape the finale, but in the "Salomon" Symphonies he relied on highly individualized and often complex sonata-rondos almost to the exclusion of other forms. Many of the finales which have contact with the sonata principle are characteristically monothematic. Once again we find a parallel in Mozart's development. As early as 1773, when Mozart first came under the influence of Haydn's *Sturm und Drang* symphonies, his finales became heavier movements that often approached the first movement in importance; part of this new importance was due to the "seriousness" acquired by the finale in its adoption of sonata form. All the last great symphonies of Mozart employ the sonata principle in the finale, though they are unlike Haydn's finales in the way they remain generally untrammelled by associations of rondo; the exceptions are the *Haffner* and *Prague* Symphonies in which the successive reappearances of the principal subject suggest a fusion of rondo with sonata form. The *Jupiter* is the finest of the true "finale symphonies", having a last movement that is not only strong and dynamic in its own right but is also adequate to the collective impetus of the foregoing movements and is the goal of the whole symphony. Its famous enlarged coda anticipates Beethoven in the way it summons yet more energy to bring the movement to its highest climax and to lead the symphony to apotheosis.

Beethoven fully realized the emancipation of the last movement and consolidated the "finale symphony". For this movement to be the dramatic focus of the whole symphony and its dénouement it was necessary that it gather to itself, either by explicit recollection or implicit reference, and always by transformation, something of the rest of the symphony; i.e. that it offer itself as in some sense the answer to the contradictions of the previous movements or, more correctly, as the accommodation of those contradictions in a synthesis on a higher dialectical plane. The most explicit recall is in the finale of the Ninth Symphony, which opens with a dramatic and unambiguous "review" of the previous momements. Another instance of overt recall is in the Fifth Symphony, where the pervasive use of the four-note motive links the finale with the first and third movements, and in which the main scherzo theme returns near the end of the development. Beethoven's finales, like the great ones of Haydn, have an individuality and an unpredictability; like those of Haydn, too, they are sometimes formal hybrids. Thus in the First Symphony the finale opens with a slow introduction, in the Second it is a baffling, subtle blend of sonata and rondo, in the Third it begins in G minor rather than in E flat major and is a variation movement, in the Eighth it is a rondo with clear suggestions of sonata, and in the Ninth a fusion of variation form with what Hans Keller has called a suppressed sonata form. Otherwise the finales are commonly sonata or rondo forms. The Beethoven finale of thematic revelations, triumphant resolutions, and a coda apotheosis, became the dominant model for the nineteenth century.

Schubert's finales, however, do not usually attempt such total and logical syntheses. His finales are not the triumphant outcome of the conflicts of the previous movements so much as a climactic assertion of the power of song to transcend those conflicts. When they do attempt a Beethoven-like victory—as in the C major conclusion to the C minor Fourth Symphony—the result, as we have pointed out, is a facile and unconvincing gesture. His finales are all sonata structures, though they tend to be still freer than his first movements. Mendelssohn's *Scotch* and *Italian* Symphonies in their own way acknowledge the Beethovenian finale. The first does so rather glibly in the way the coda suggests a culmination and release from dualism by the introduction of a new periodic and hymnic melody in an *allegro moderato assai* tempo. The *Italian*, on the other hand, has considerably more originality. Its procedure is based on a full inversion of the Beethoven ethic of victory: it ends not with a cumulative outburst but in defeat, running down despairingly as if from exhaustion; it is one of the first symphonies to allow the Beethovenian principle of conflict to issue in failure instead of triumph. Both these finales are sonata forms; that in the *Italian* is also more interesting for its technique of suggesting dramatic progress by substituting new material for the old at the second-subject stage of the recapitulation and amalgamating this with coda function.

Sharing Mendelssohn's lack of a full mastery of the Classical dialectical method and of Beethoven's technique of significant transformation, Schumann sometimes also harnessed a new theme to the coda to clinch the dramatic resolution—such as he occasionally did in codas to other movements as well. In the Second Symphony the coda theme is hinted at earlier in the movement, and in the Fourth the rousing, climactic new theme drives the coda ever quicker to its end. The coda of the Third Symphony is more subtle in that the discovery in the development of a triadic *Urthema* which obtains for the whole symphony, but sounds like new material, is used together with other thematic resolutions, and recollections of earlier parts of the symphony, to build the coda to a great climax. All Schumann's finales are sonata forms; among their individualities are the use of a slow introduction in the Fourth Symphony, the omission of the first subject from the recapitulation in the same movement, and the dovetailing of development and recapitulation in the Second Symphony.

If Brahms grew ever less able to write a Beethovenian finale of triumph it was not for want of technique—which he had in abundance—but for reasons which have something to do with his having been born in 1833 rather than 1770. Only in the First Symphony did Brahms attempt to recreate and inhabit Beethoven's world of heroism. There the finale's allegro emerges triumphantly in C major out of the troubled C minor adagio which introduces it, and puts down attempts to undermine it before culminating in the apotheosis of the coda. By the Third Symphony the change is marked. In the finale, the second subject's C major opposition to the F minor first subject has a facile optimism. It cannot triumph, as the sostenuto coda reveals when it slowly loses energy and momentum, and dissolves the movement into an ethereal, sighed remembrance of the once strenuous and impassioned opening theme of the first movement. This is thematic resolution indeed, but it is not a fulfilment of the heroic aspirations of the rest of the symphony. There is no triumph, only resignation to the fact that the Beethoven world of achievement is unattainable. In the Fourth Symphony the change is complete. The finale is still the climax, focal point, and resolution of the symphony, but now in formal, stoical terms; dualism finds synthesis in the monism of a profound and laconic passacaglia.

The finales of Berlioz are in many ways the most unconventional we have so far encountered, though whatever else happens they still retain a sense of essential dramatic completion and climax. The "*Songe d'une nuit du Sabbat*" in the *Symphonie Fantastique* is an unusual type of through-composed sectional form, starting with a larghetto introduction. The movement realizes the "destiny" of the thematic lives of the symphony, and does so in terms of a triumph which is a perversion—or inversion—of the Beethoven model: if it is a victory it is a diabolical one. In this way the work has some relation to Mendelssohn's *Italian* Symphony, and also—though much less—to Brahms's Third. The reminiscences of former movements at the beginning of the finale of *Harold* have an immediate precedent in Beethoven's Ninth Symphony. But the movement, though preserving a sonata "shape", is static and ritornello-like; it uses a recapitulation that is absolutely identical with the exposition, a departure from dynamic principles that is not redeemed by a second quasi-development in the coda. (This postponed development is a procedure that recalls but does not repeat the success of the first movement of the *Symphonie Fantastique*). The coda replaces G minor with G major. As for the symphonic poem, we indicated in our earlier discussions that Liszt and Strauss made it a single-movement synthesis of the multi-movement traditional symphony; we need therefore only remind ourselves that we saw there that the symphonic poem pursued a "symphonic" notion of thematic "destiny", and that this could end in an inversion, as well as in a preservation, of the Beethovenian finale ideal.

It is to Bruckner yet again that we have to look to find the most explicitly intended and most fully realized Beethovenian finales of the nineteenth century. These finales accept the contrasts of the previous movements in all their complexity and attempt no less than their total synthesis. Sometimes, as sometimes also in Beethoven, part of the machinery of this process is apparent: in the Eighth Symphony, for instance, the principal subjects of the first two movements are recalled near the end of the movement, and then, for the last thirteen bars of the work, the main ideas of all four movements appear simultaneously, resolved triumphantly over a C major common chord. Other explicit recollections occur in the codas of the Third and Seventh Symphonies; and nearly all the finales embody at some stage veiled reference to previous movements. The Fifth Symphony follows the example of Beethoven's Ninth in beginning its finale with a review of themes from earlier (in this case the first two) movements. Generally too the finales involve their first movements by a structural and thematic affinity with them. All reach glorious major-key apotheoses.

Formally the finales are highly sophisticated sonata structures showing the same types of peculiarity as the first movements, but connecting with a long tradition in their architectural freedom and individuality, and their resistence to categorization; it is even more true of the finales than of the first movements that they are composed against, rather than in, sonata form. One of the most interesting of the movements is in the Fifth Symphony: there sonata achieves synthesis with a fugue on three subjects in a finale whose general precedents are to be found in Haydn and Mozart, but above all in the late works of Beethoven.

Dvořák's finales operate within a fairly conservative framework. Sonata forms are common; an interesting exception is the Eighth Symphony which has as its finale a theme and a series of variations amounting to a broadly ternary form. The finale of the Fifth Symphony begins in the "wrong" key of A minor before moving eventually to the "correct" F major—a procedure which we will remember was used by Beethoven, and later also by others (for instance by Bruckner, in his Eighth Symphony). Dvořák's finales favour recalling, either explicitly or in the partial guise of a "new" theme, the first subject of the opening movement. But nowhere are the recollections more thorough than in the Ninth Symphony where the coda confirms the "discoveries" of the development that we spoke of earlier (see page 53), and interweaves the principal subjects of all four movements and the introduction to the second.

Tchaikovsky's finales make two important innovations: the Sixth Symphony has an adagio for a finale, and the Third a polonaise. (Balakirev's First Symphony has a finale coda in *tempo di polacca*). In the Sixth Symphony we have another instance of the type that connects with the Beethovenian ideal by inverting it. Instead of a final winning through to apotheosis, this last movement submits to a final catastrophe: the second subject, an opposition to the first subject in the symphony's prevailing opposition key of D major, collapses cataclysmically and hurtles downwards through a stringendo string passage into the finally ineluctable main key of B minor. There are anticipations of this inescapable tragedy elsewhere in Tchaikovsky's symphonies. It lurks in the Fourth, for example, but there it is up to a point simply evaded: just before the coda in the finale the first movement's fateful fanfare intrudes, insisting that the high spirits of the movement are no final answer to it—but then the symphony merely picks up its former manner and escapes into the exhilarating coda. Sonata form finales are common in Russian symphonies in the last third of the nineteenth century.

V

This brief history of the pre-twentieth-century symphony is

at an end. The study of a century-and-a-half of symphonic writing shows how the forces of renewal, operating between the poles of strong conservation and imaginative reinterpretation, transmitted the Classical symphony and particularly its Beethovenian manifestation through the nineteenth century and brought it, still a living organism, to the dawn of the twentieth. We are now ready to turn to the twentieth century and to try to understand the nature of some of the symphonic developments that have taken place in it.

NOTES

[1] This view of a specific tonality as a kind of *Weltanschauung* in which the tonic is the centre that holds together and orders a particular set of entities is by no means new; c.f., for example, Furtwängler: "Tonality, in which each note is referred to the whole range of human emotion, and man, as listener, is unreservedly made the centre of the whole, corresponds to the anthropomorphic, ptolemaic-Christian view of the world." (*Concerning Music*, p. 93).

[2] *The Keyboard Music of C. P. E. Bach*, London 1965, p. 83. I have explored and developed these philosophical implications in my "Beethoven, Hegel and Marx", *Music Review*, Vol. 33, No. 1, Feb. 1972, pp. 34–46.

[3] *Wöchentliche Nachrichten*, 1768, p. 107. Quoted by Lang, Paul Henry; *Music in Western Civilisation*, p. 589.

[4] Throughout this study various terms are used for what are here called "groups": the criterion is that of appropriateness.

[5] *The Thematic Process in Music*; see especially p. 60.

[6] *Style and Idea*, London 1951, p. 211.

[7] *op. cit.*, p. 60.

[8] *op. cit.*, p. 212.

[9] *op. cit.*, pp. 28–29.

[10] *Beethoven*, p. 71.

[11] *ibid.*, p. 76.

[12] *op. cit.*, pp. 29–30. This change from the Baroque to the Classical style is discussed from a more philosophical point of view in my "Beethoven, Hegel and Marx", *loc. cit.*

[13] *Mozart: His Character, his Work*, p. 215.

[14] Quoted by Thayer, Alexander Wheelock (tr. H. E. Krehbiel); *Life of Beethoven*, 2 vols., Princeton (rev.), 1967, Vol. II, p. 43.

[15] *A Critical Study of Beethoven's Symphonies* (tr. E. Evans), London N.D., p. 66.

[16] *op. cit.*, see especially pp. 157–160.

[17] *ibid*, p. 157.

[18] *Music in our Time*, p. 93 f.

[19] See Basil Lam in *The Symphony* (ed. Simpson, Robert), Vol. I, pp. 141–142.

[20] For instance, in a letter in June, 1838, Schumann called the Ninth Symphony "the most important work in instrumental music in recent times."

[21] From his essay on Schubert's Ninth Symphony (1840). Quoted by Pleasants, Henry; *The Musical World of Robert Schumann*; a *Selection from his own Writings*, London 1965, p. 164.

[22] Quoted by Pleasants, *op. cit.*, p. 148.

[23] The First Symphony also has contrasts that are on the whole less generative than those in Classical times, but for a rather different reason—namely that the contrasts are diverting rather than dramatic, and are less than crucial aspects of the structure. The symphony is not a single, powerful span in which contrasts support each other and regulate the structure. The motto theme in this context is clearly a conscious attempt to provide unification to the weakened span.

[24] See for instance Latham, Peter; *Brahms*, p. 102.

[25] *op. cit.*, pp. 163–164.

[26] *Memoirs of Hector Berlioz* (tr. Rachel and Eleanor Holmes), London 1966, p. 76.

[27] *ibid.*, p. 487.

[28] *Hector Berlioz*, London ,1935 p. 156.

[29] *Berlioz and the Romantic Century*, Vol. I, p. 155.

[30] *ibid.*, Vol. I, p. 338.

[31] Dickinson, A. E. F.; *Vaughan Williams*, p. 182.

[32] *Beethoven et ses trois styles*, St. Petersburg, 1852.

[33] La Mara (ed.); *Letters of Franz Liszt* (tr. C. Bach), 2 vols., London 1894, Vol. I, pp. 151–152.

[34] *Bogen* = literally, "bow". German theorists, of whom the first appears to have been Alfred Lorenz, have used this term to describe a more or less modern development of ternary form. Liszt's *Hamlet*, represented by ABC D CBA, shows the idea excellently: see Gerald Abraham, *A Hundred Years of Music*, p. 39.

[35] In his preface to Scherchen, Hermann; *The Nature of Music*, p. 10.

[36] For the sake of succinctness my quotations are taken from Gerald Abraham's excellent summary of *Oper und Drama* in his *A Hundred Years of Music*. His direct quotations from the work, which I have retained in their inverted commas, were taken or adapted from the translation by Edwin Evans, Senior, in *Opera and Drama*, London, N.D. The present quotation is from Abraham, pp. 99–100.

[37] *ibid.*, p. 106.

[38] *ibid.*, p. 107.

[39] Schuh, Willi, and Trenner, Franz (eds.); *Hans von Bülow and Richard Strauss: Correspondence*, (trs. A. Goshford), London 1955, pp. 81–82.

[40] Quoted by Krause, Ernst; *Richard Strauss: the Man and his Work*, p. 219.

[41] See his *An Historical Approach to Musical Form*, pp. 155–157.

[42] See Specht, Richard; *Richard Strauss und sein Werk*, 2 vols., Leipzig 1921. See also Del Mar, Norman; *Richard Strauss: A Critical Commentary on his Life and Work*, p. 166.

[43] *The Essence of Bruckner*, pp. 198–199.

[44] Tchaikovsky, Modeste; *Life and Letters of Peter Ilyich Tchaikovsky*, (tr. R. Newmarch), New York N.D., p. 311.

[45] *ibid.*, p. 294.

[46] *ibid.*, pp. 292–294.

[47] *A Study in Musical Analysis*, pp. 116–126.

[48] In *The Symphony, op. cit.*, Vol. I, p. 346.

[49] This, and related aspects, is well discussed in Gerald Abraham's *Studies in Russian Music*, p. 102f, and his *On Russian Music*, p. 179 f.

[50] Strictly speaking the dominant is a less orthodox choice here than, say, the relative would have been, for the work is in a minor key.

[51] *Bruckner, Mahler, Schoenberg*, pp. 85–88.

Part Two
The Twentieth Century: Innovation in "Form"

2

Conservative structural innovation in the symphony

I

At this point survey ends. No longer shall we be concerned with an attempt to be anything like "comprehensive". Nevertheless, in our way of proceeding we will try to be as logical as possible. We move on now directly to an examination of twentieth-century symphonies that preserve conventional forms but begin to depart moderately— yet significantly—from them. Works that are "wholly" conventional in structure will not be dealt with, for the obvious reason that, since they add very little to our knowledge of what a symphony might be, they belong to a general survey rather than to a limited study of the continuing evolution of the symphony in the twentieth century.

In this chapter, then, we shall be concerned with symphonic features that carry on progressive developments, or that extrapolate from hints in earlier symphonic practice, or that are themselves quite novel—but always with the limitation that none of these developments will go so far as to seem to call into question the existence of a relationship with some well-founded aspect of traditional symphonic practice. We shall be concerned with developments made on the basis of this practice, rather than with radical departures from it: that is why we can speak of "moderate" innovations. In addition to this, one further limitation—and a crucial one—is implied. It is that the works to which these moderately innovatory features belong, and which are cited as examples, are still "conceptually" symphonic in the sense running through this entire study: namely, they are essentially and definitively preoccupied with the traditional problem of *sonata dualism*.

II

With the weakening or disappearance of tonality as a structuring element, composers have looked for other ways to control their material. One procedure that has suggested itself has been to divide what might otherwise have been a single complex movement into two or more movements; or put differently, to strengthen the bond between separate symphonic movements by maintaining between two or more of them some affinity of style, idiom, or character. This is done over and above the usual fundamental thematic unity that can be taken for granted in most symphonies.

The genre of the scherzo seems to lend itself well to this kind of treatment: and there is of course a famous precedent (mentioned earlier—see page 69) in the *Symphonie Fantastique*. Mahler's Ninth Symphony, for instance, like say, his Third, spreads a general "scherzo" style over two of its movements (movements two and three). The first of these is a *Ländler* with two consecutive trios, and the second the defiant and savagely parodistic *Rondo Burlesque*. And there is an intimate dramatic and temporal connection between these two movements that reinforces our sense of their being, from one point of view, a single complex movement written as two. The *Ländler* had begun as an attempt, through the symbol of the dance, to recreate the vanishing world that was so much the cause of the first movement's conflict. But the vision of the old world did not come easily; the picture was distorted. Diatonicism became overloaded with chromaticism and by the imminence of other tonal centres; tonality frequently seemed on the point of breaking down. The mood of the movement became increasingly hysterical, and the distorted, conjured-up world faded before our eyes in the coda: thus the bitter parody, the grotesquely reductive view, of the *Rondo Burlesque*.

A somewhat similar state of affairs obtains in Shostakovich's Eighth Symphony. Like Mahler, Shostakovich spreads a scherzo character over movements two and three, and adopts the common scherzo-and-trio form only in the first of them. But unlike the Mahler of the Ninth Symphony, he places the second scherzo movement in abrupt and powerful contrast to its companion piece. In the first scherzo movement, despite the orthodox form, there is no mere literal repetition, and the whole grows spontaneously to a central climax. But the quicker second scherzo is a dogged and imperturbable movement of amazing symmetry: a ternary form in which a militaristic and tuneful central section is framed by a trenchant *moto perpetuo* of compelling regularity. The contrast is obvious; yet in a long work of fierce conflicts, two of the central movements are drawn together (despite the duality between them) by this affinity of genre. The procedure here is very similar to that in the second and third movements of Mahler's Second Symphony.

One also finds a symphonic scherzo divided into three movements. In that probably unique synthesis of symphony and song cycle, Mahler's *Das Lied von der Erde*,[1] movements three, four and five ("*Von der Jugend*", "*Von der Schönheit*", and "*Der Trunkene im Frühling*") may be taken together for they quite obviously share affinities of mood, and concern themselves with some of life's pleasures—youth, beauty and intoxication by wine and by spring. They stand collectively in sharp contrast to the other movements of the work, textually and musically. They are predominantly major in key, bright-toned, lively, uninhibitedly happy; they are also all relatively short. It is thus fair to see their function in terms of the symphony as a whole as that of a "multiple scherzo".

Movements other than scherzo may also be subdivided. Mahler provides felicitous instances here too. In the Third Symphony, the fourth and fifth movements obviously fall together through being the only vocal movements in the symphony and through the way they complement each other by speaking respectively of the grief and longing of the human soul, and of eternal paradise. In the very vigorous Fifth Symphony, the traditional first movement is subdivided into two separate movements which together make up what Mahler delineates as Part 1. The first of these presents the material: the second takes it up, nearly in its original form or otherwise in varied form, and develops it. Here the method of splitting up a single movement into a multiple movement clearly gives Mahler a way of controlling his material. It is a principle of restraint, wholly in keeping with the neo-Classical disposition of the work. The first part of the multiple movement is a *Trauermarsch* in C sharp minor and straightforward rondo form; the second part, in which the moods of the first are largely unrelieved, is a complex fusion of rondo, sonata, and variation forms.

So far all the movement sub-divisions we have seen have resulted in a multiplicity of consecutive or conjunct movements. This is the obvious solution; but there would appear to be no reason why a disjunct placing could not result: i.e. one in which the various "parts" were separated by a different movement altogether. Indeed Mahler's Seventh Symphony provides an instance of this. Both the slow movements are titled *Nachtmusik*, suggesting different parts of a multiple movement. But they occur as movements two and four in the five-movement work, are situated respectively in C minor and F Major, and are separated by a sinister *schattenhaft* (ghostly) scherzo in D minor.

Another controlling, form-giving operation sometimes used by symphonists of the twentieth century is the combination, within a single movement, of two (or more) structural principles. Thus, for instance, sonata organization is added to variation forms, to scherzo movements, to rondos, and is synthesised with fugues; variation principle is united with rondo or ternary shapes; and so on.

Let us look at some examples. The first movement of Vaughan Williams's Eighth Symphony is a complex synthesis of monistic variation form and orthodox dualistic sonata structure. An initial complication is that the movement (called "Fantasia") is a series of *variazioni senza tema*: there are no unambiguously stated thematic "positives". One important consequence for the inherent

sonata structure follows from this: in the absence of any
absolute point of reference, such dualistic oppositions as
there are, are free to define themselves anew continually;
the opposing tendencies in the music are differently
characterized at different times. The two opening variations
belong together, the first introducing material that the
second subjects to some development. If the latter is rapid,
diabolic, chromatic, and with prickly syncopation, the third
variation (*andante sostenuto* and C major) is precisely and
dramatically the opposite. This cantabile section arrives
with the force of a second group of a sonata exposition—
which in terms of the inherent sonata structure is exactly
what it is. From the sonata viewpoint, the fourth and fifth
variations are the development section, the former
developing mainly the first variation, and the latter mainly
the third. The development seems to overflow into the sixth
variation. But this section is also a revision of the second
variation; and when it breaks off suddenly (as it did in the
"exposition") and is followed by the affirmative seventh
variation, an *andante sostenuto* and a varied return of the
third, we realize that the movement is in the process of
recapitulating. Furthermore, in Beethoven-like fashion the
music has grown through conflict, and swells into a glorious
largamente passage in D major. The slow movement of
Mahler's Fourth Symphony might likewise be considered as
basically a set of variations compounded with sonata
organization.

Various possibilities exist for the fusion of sonata form
with scherzo structures. For a start the trio may be treated
as a second subject—a procedure used in Schumann's Third
Symphony and adopted by Vaughan Williams perhaps
most notably in his Sixth Symphony. Here, as so often with
symphonic movements that bring together and unite
different forms, any "simpler" view of the movement will
fail to do justice to its complexity. The description of the
Vaughan Williams movement given by most analysts—
simply as a scherzo with a trio that returns after an
expanded reprise—wholly misses the dynamic, evolving
nature of the movement, its dramatic nature, and the fact
that it has the most extensive and the most classical

development in the whole work. A more adequate view would see the opening scherzo section (mainly on a B flat tonic) as being simultaneously the first group, and the trio (setting out in C minor) as the second group. The scherzo repeat is then the development—though only of the first group—which initiates a varied, abbreviated recapitulation; and the reprise of the second subject is traditional in this sense also, that there is now much less differentiation between it and the first group, since the heavy texture and the fortissimo dynamic level are maintained. The scherzo (titled "Humoreske") of Nielsen's Sixth Symphony behaves fairly similarly, the chief exception being that it forgoes recapitulation after a quasi-development. Closer to the formal technique of the scherzo of Vaughan Williams's Sixth is the scherzo of the Third Symphony by Charles Ives. The movement is a splendid amalgam: not only does Ives manage to develop both "subjects" (the second within the boundaries of the trio), but contrives also to turn the trio into a sonata structure that is fully developed except for a recapitulation!

Just as Ives treats the trio as an "independent" sonata form, so also the scherzo section may be treated in such a way. Indeed, this manner was implicit in many nineteenth-century scherzos (Bruckner's for example) and it is an idea that bears fruit in the twentieth century. The Second and Fourth Symphonies of Vaughan Williams, for instance, add sonata procedures to their scherzo movements by using this technique; but a more intricate development of this idea is that worked out by Mahler in the scherzo of his Fifth Symphony. The following schema may suggest this intricacy:

A: D major. Sonata exposition and a terse development but no recapitulation: only a brief closing theme. The section ends in D major.

B: B flat major. Another sharp contrast—the first trio, a gentle *Ländler*.

A: D major again, initially. A counter-exposition, with another development. Also acts as a transition by anticipating the themes of the next section.

88

C: D minor. The second trio—another *Ländler*. (Followed by a Classical development of principal elements from A, B, and C: the dramatic crisis of the movement).

A: D major. General recapitulation of principal elements of the movement, all grafted onto a predominantly "A" (i.e. scherzo) section.

Coda.

This movement thus also contains a rondo shape (ABACA); and one might perhaps do the piece equal justice by explaining it as a rondo organization of a scherzo-and-trio movement, pressed into the service of sonata. As such, the complexity may be new, but the appropriation of sonata thought by rondo form has of course a long history. We must note that those two forms (rondo and sonata) offer nevertheless another opportunity of formal combination to twentieth-century symphonists. Indeed, the second movement of the same Mahler Symphony fuses modified rondo form (ABABABCAB) with sonata form (AB, exposition); ABAB, development; C, interpolation or episode; AB, recapitulation). More novel and intriguing syntheses of rondo and sonata forms are those systematically explored by Fricker throughout his Second Symphony. A special interest of these syntheses is the occasional incompatibility, or at least incongruity, of the two forms—where the sectional boundaries of the different forms do not coincide, but rather overlap. The final movement, for example, has a striking instance of tension between parallel rondo and sonata forms. The first section (i.e. group) which is of course also the refrain of the rondo, propels itself to a tonic D just before cue 5, and then gives way to what may be taken to be the second section, or the rondo's first episode. But at cue 8 the momentum of this section is punctuated by three brisk chords, drawing attention to what then suggests itself to be the beginning of the sonata form development—especially as it starts in a different (meno mosso) tempo and after six bars recalls the introduction to the movement. In rondo terms, however, this is felt to be merely an interpolation, for the music now reveals itself as an extension of what has gone before—i.e. the first episode. Neither in mood, style, orchestration, or thematic identity does it differ seriously from that first episode. What has happened in fact, is that the sonata form has thrown its development right across this expansive first episode and has done so emphatically, with a heavily stressed end to the exposition and start of the development. A great structural tension results from this disjunct correlation of the two forms.

One further amalgam involving sonata is worth mentioning: the combination of sonata with fugue. An impressive case is the finale of the Sixth Symphony by Karl Amadeus Hartmann, which as a sonata finale on three fugues has a notable precedent in Bruckner's Fifth Symphony. Hartmann's finale, however, is perhaps more easily assimilable to traditional sonata outline than is Bruckner's: in the twentieth-century work, the three fugues correspond broadly to exposition, development, and re-capitulation. Simplest is the first fugue, which counts as exposition if only because it provides the material for the whole movement. The second fugue simulates development by fracturing and fragmenting its original lines and by using other orthodox developmental techniques; it is also the central pillar of the movement. The third fugue is recapitulatory insofar that it approximates its subject closely to that of the first fugue. Less throughgoing is Walton's approach in the finale of his First Symphony: here fugue is confined to the second subject of the exposition, and to parts of the development.

All the synthetic forms we have examined so far have involved sonata organization of some kind: i.e. as one of their components. Though these would appear to be the most interesting type of amalgams, others do occur in symphonic writing—combinations involving variation principle, for example. We have already seen fusions of variation and sonata; brief mention might be made of two other types. Rondo and variation is a felicitous combination, much favoured by Mahler. The Fifth Symphony is permeated by this union; the Seventh adopts it in movements two and five. Its convenience in these works seems to be that it allows the composer to make use of the strongly unifying technique of repetition and at the same time enables him to avoid straightforward reiteration by creating an evolving thematic network. Or variation technique may be combined with, say, ternary form, as happens in the slow movement of Prokofiev's Seventh Symphony.

III

Among the problems facing twentieth-century symphonists disposed to make use of orthodox form, is the problem of recapitulation. In the Classical era there was a patent musical logic at work within structural repetition: indeed, the two procedures—repetition and logical continuation—were really inseparable, for they both stemmed from the formal Classical aesthetic. This unity (as we saw in Chapter 1) became problematic after the Classical age proper, as music began to demand new kinds of structure—often as a consequence of the unfolding in the music of an explicit symbolic (or even programmatic) content. This problem persists into the twentieth century; but its solution seems to be somewhat simpler now, since symphonic composers apparently have fewer scruples about bending orthodox form to suit their needs, and even forgoing recapitulation altogether when necessary.

A particularly notable case of a "musico-dramatic" situation rendering formal reprise not merely redundant but actually "impossible", is the scherzo of Sibelius's Fourth Symphony. Throughout this work the interval of the tritone plays a highly disruptive role; in the scherzo, it begins to work its corruption in the *doppio piu lento* section. This is generically the trio; it has no stable tonality, but B, the key tritonally distant from the home tonic (F), offers itself strongly as a potential tonal centre. F and B now lock in a fruitless, annihilating strife that soon brings the movement to an end. At the conclusion all that is left of the original material is the merest ghost of the first theme, which flickers to life within the domain of B and is promptly smothered, and a vague memory of the principal tonic, struck lifelessly upon timpani soli. These are also all that remain of the spirit of reprise that in a classical work would have brought back the first part of the scherzo at this point. Here no return is possible—perhaps because no pre-established order has meaning in the face of such internal conflicts. This movement omits reprise from a scherzo-and-trio form; the slow movement of Nielsen's Fourth Symphony (*The Inextinguishable*) omits reprise from a sonata structure—and for similar "dramatic" reasons. The first subject begins as a writhing string line, with a desiccated timpani and pizzicato accompaniment that is brilliantly macabre; the contrasting second subject has a disarming simplicity. These meet in contrapuntal combat in the development; when the second theme has found an ostinato to match that of the first, the battle freezes into stability. There is no recapitulation: both themes are spent, and in the ensuing relative calm motives from them fly about fragmentarily. A somewhat different "dramatic" situation occurs in the finale of Honegger's *Symphonie Liturgique*: here it is not that after sonata conflict there is not enough energy for recapitulation, but rather that there is, in a sense, too much: the apotheosis within reach after the development is of a kind of "other-worldiness", realized by a slow hymnic epilogue situated in the relative of the dominant of the symphony's principal tonal centre.

Sometimes only a part of the recapitulation is rendered "dramatically" superfluous and thus omitted. In the sonata-form finale of Shostakovich's Fifth Symphony there is no second-group reprise: in leading from recapitulatory hesitancy to an ultimate and triumphant solution of its "problems", and those of the symphony, the first group has superseded the majestic second; for the second group to return now would be gratuitous and formalistic. Much the same takes place in the finale of the same composer's Seventh Symphony. How successful—indeed how necessary—such measures are in symphonies with a certain type of dramatic content, may be inferred from works which fail to make a sufficient amendment to their recapitulation when this seems called for. An example is the first movement of Mahler's Third Symphony, which suffers from a contradiction between a fluid exposition that takes shape under dramatic—perhaps even programmatic—forces, and a somewhat formalistic recapitulation. "My work", said Mahler, in a letter to Anna von Milderburg, in July 1896, "is a musical poem embracing all stages of development in a progressive order; it begins with inanimate nature and rises to the love of God!" The first movement poses a conflict between the first-subject complex—a symbol for Mahler's "inanimate nature"—and the second-subject complex, which symbolises the life-force of "summer marching in", and finally triumphs over the first group. In the exposition the themes take shape slowly, dramatically, interacting constantly; after this formal freedom the recapitulation—despite abbreviation—sounds stiff and contrived, a formalistic reprise in an otherwise freely and dynamically generative movement.

At the same time, recapitulation may be truncated or omitted for reasons which have nothing to do with any overt "dramatic" or symbolic significance. Britten's Cello Symphony has a sonata-form third movement that forsakes recapitulation of its second group apparently in order to be able to bring it back, transformed, as the main theme of the linked final movement: this certainly results in fine formal integration. The finale of Walton's First Symphony recapitulates no more than the grand preface which opened the movement; the first subject is there only by implication.

None of our examples of varied recapitulation has come from a symphonic first movement. This may perhaps indicate—though it is impossible to be sure—that composers have a freer attitude to recapitulation in later movements than they do in first movements; however, it should not suggest that first movements are quite exempt from this kind of treatment. Two of the works cited (Sibelius's Fourth Symphony and Walton's First) do in fact in their first movements forgo a reprise of the second subject; and in a work such as Copland's Second (*Short*) Symphony, recapitulation is forfeited altogether in each of the three movements—or at best merely suggested.

A further liberty with sonata form sometimes taken by

twentieth-century composers is a breaking down, by various means, of any too firm boundaries between development and other sections of the movement—for instance, between development and exposition. Developmental tendencies existed of course within "non-developmental" sections of Classical and nineteenth-century sonata structures—between or after formal thematic statements, for instance; some twentieth-century symphonists have built upon this tradition, with the result often of blurring the definition of separate sections.

Walton's First Symphony approaches this condition in its outer movements by making working-out integral to much of the music's progress. Thus in the first movement, apart from the greater number of keys that are passed through, and a greater concentration of certain motives, there is nothing fundamentally different between the "official" development section and other sections of the movement. And in the finale, the first subject exposes a good number of its developmental possibilities *before* the second subject arrives. Similarly, in the finale of Shostakovich's Fifth Symphony, the first group ventures into an 80-bar development almost at once: it is unshakable once it has started developing, and the second group, in order to make itself heard, has simply to interrupt. Even then the first full statement of that group does not take place until some bars later—the time it takes for the orchestra to be brought under control and gradually fixed to the dominant of the second group's approaching tonality.

Nielsen, in the first movement of his Sixth Symphony, vests this procedure with the special significance that the second group appears as a *consequence* of the first-group development: it is a "discovery" about that first group.[2] The finale of Shostakovich's Seventh Symphony "displaces" development not only by interposing it between the exposition of the subjects, but also by "postponing" it so that it occurs simultaneously with the recapitulation of the first group. From one point of view the latter amounts to a dovetailing of development and recapitulation—a synthesis mastered by Bruckner and frequently achieved in the twentieth century (the first movement of Shostakovich's

Tenth and the finale of Stravinsky's Symphony in C are other instances).

Of course the displacement of development in that Shostakovich finale—as in some of our other examples—means that we can actually speak of two developments. And if two are possible, then why not more? Indeed, the scherzo of Mahler's Fifth Symphony has three. If we refer back to our analysis of this movement—which we understood as a scherzo-and-trio form grafted onto a sonata structure (page 88)—we shall see that development occurs in the first scherzo section (sonata exposition and development), in the second scherzo section (counter-exposition and development), and after the second trio (a general development).

A few other modifications to sonata form are worth mentioning. Composers of large-scale symphonies some-times take note of Bruckner's example and make use of three themes (for instance, the finale of Elgar's Second and Shostakovich's Eighth, the first movement of Copland's Third, and possibly the first movement of Walton's First). On the other hand, a composer may reduce his thematic field by dispensing with the second subject. This is partially true of the first movement of Mahler's First Symphony, where technically there is no second subject; however, Mahler maintains a semblance of formal orthodoxy by treating the *langsam* introduction as a kind of first group and allowing it to return in the development. But it is certainly true of the first movement of Sibelius's Sixth Symphony (like the one-movement Seventh): here even the outline of an alternative subject is abandoned. Indeed, it is worth pointing out that to speak even of a "first subject" would be invalid and merely academic, since Sibelius's germinal procedure is too fluid and consistently rapid to allow any fragment the prerogative of such a term. Yet this does not mean that Sibelius has forgone any interest in dualism—only that he has found new ways to bring it about, as we shall see in a later chapter.

But to return to Mahler: as long ago as Haydn, composers would occasionally allow a slow introduction to make a dramatic return during a movement: this broadly is

Mahler's precedent, in the example mentioned. However, as the Mahler example implies, modern symphonic practice may also intensify this procedure. A good example is Honegger's *Symphonie pour Orchestre à Cordes*. In this work the first movement formally elevates the slow introduction to the status of a fully active participant in the drama; it features in development and recapitulation, playing the role of an "extra" subject in addition to the normal two. Or almost: in the greatly abbreviated recapitulation the introduction and second subject recur simultaneously; thus retrospectively they are felt as having been disjunct parts of the same whole, parts that the development helped to unite. (Appropriately the aggressive first subject, which was the principal factor in their separation, has its reprise relegated to the very end of the movement; it is now also subdued).

IV

During the present discussion, many of our examples have been provided by scherzo movements. This movement, to be sure, had a history of some eccentricity even before the twentieth century; and we must now take stock of some of the ways in which modern composers have extended and developed this tradition. Schumann's use of two dissimilar trios finds an echo in, say, Mahler's Ninth Symphony, where the difference between the trios is further sharpened: the first is a waltz, the second a minuet. Besides, the formal deployment of these sections is rather unexpected. The scherzo (a *Ländler*) does not return immediately after the first trio, for this is followed directly by the second trio, and then both are repeated; only after this does the principal section return, as a reprise which eventually gives way to another hearing of the first trio.

The use of dissimilar trios may bring a movement very close to rondo form—how close is suggested by the scherzo of Vaughan Williams's Fifth Symphony, where the movement is open to two formal descriptions: as either a rondo, or (thinking generically) a scherzo with two closely related but dissimilar trios. This perhaps rationalizes the use of unambiguous rondo forms by scherzo movements—such as that in Walton's First Symphony, Tippett's Second, and the "*Rondo Burlesque*" in Mahler's Ninth. Similarly, the older, orthodox minuet-and-trio form in which a single trio occupied the central position in the movement, may argue a genealogy for simple ternary form (ABA) when this appears in scherzo movements—as it does, for instance, in Shostakovich's Eighth Symphony (third movement), or in the Sixth Symphony by Egon Wellesz. By the same token, scherzos in extended ternary form (ABABA) hint at an affiliation to, say, those Beethoven movements that place *two* statements of a single trio between three of the scherzo section: when that kind of extended ternary scherzo appears in a work as Classically oriented as Prokofiev's Seventh Symphony, the affiliation seems still stronger.

At the same time, there is at least one twentieth-century movement of decidedly scherzo origin written in a binary form; this is the third movement of Sibelius's Sixth Symphony, and one is tempted to describe it as a scherzo without the typical trio. More novel still, but founded nevertheless upon a firm historical foundation, is the scherzo of Stravinsky's Symphony in C, a movement described by the composer himself as a suite of dances. Implicitly Stravinsky has here gone back further than the symphonic scherzo, beyond even the symphonic minuet out of which it grew, to its antecedent, the dance suite. There are four well-defined sections; easy correspondences to conventional dance styles are, however, not readily forthcoming. Even further (but not for the same reason) from the Classical formal movement, is the generic scherzo movement of Britten's Symphony for Cello and Orchestra—a presto in triple metre, organized as a set of free variations. And the scherzo "movement" of the formally very complex Fifth Symphony by Nielsen is a fugue.

Another—and a fairly common—species of scherzo arrangement has already been dealt with: that involving some sort of amalgam of scherzo-and-trio form with sonata form. Vaughan Williams, Mahler, and Ives were cited. We need now to take note of the further fact that sometimes composers write sonata-principle scherzos without there being any simultaneous presence of conventional scherzo-and-trio form. For example, the third movement of Nielsen's Third (*Espansiva*) Symphony is a Brahmsian allegretto scherzo set in a fairly straightforward sonata form; Shostakovich's Fourth Symphony has a sonata-form *Ländler* movement; and the scherzo movement of Elgar's Second Symphony is a weighty sonata-rondo.

V

So far we have discussed moderate *structural* developments in twentieth-century symphonies. But there is another type of moderate development, perhaps linked sometimes to a structural change, but observable chiefly as a change in the *character*, *style* or *function* of a movement or other component of a symphony. We begin with a rather minor instance, but one following on directly from our discussion of the scherzo. In the nineteenth century, composers occasionally wrote a scherzo in something other than the usual triple metre; in such cases a duple metre was commonly taken. Twentieth-century symphonists do much the same, though apparently more frequently. Whenever this happens, of course, the scherzo undergoes a slight change of character. Among modern symphonies having duple-metre scherzos are the Eighth of Vaughan Williams and Shostakovich (in the second of its two scherzos), and the Fourth of Prokofiev, Martinů, and Franz Schmidt; among those with quadruple-metre scherzos are Prokofiev's Fifth, Shostakovich's First and his Eighth (first scherzo). Or the metre may fluctuate, as in Shostakovich's Seventh and Twelfth, and Stravinsky's Symphony in C. A change in the expected tempo of a particular movement can have an effect more surprising than a metrical change; and in the twentieth century a movement quite often written outside of its normal fastish tempo is the first. Slow first movements occur for example in Mahler's Ninth, Shostakovich's Eighth, Wellesz's Sixth, and Karl Amadeus Hartmann's Sixth.

More far-reaching still is the removal of dualism from the

first movement and its postponement to the second or even a later movement. Mahler's First Symphony is an example. But for a single, fleeting suggestion near the end of the development, dualism is banished from the first movement. This is no doubt a consequence of Mahler's avoidance of a real second subject. It is true, as we have seen, that Mahler elevates the introduction to the status of a kind of independent group, but there is no dualistic import between these "groups": both involve the tonic D and do not pretend to any thematic opposition. Only in the finale are the conflicts fully presented and played out. Another work which broaches conflict at a very late stage is Copland's First Symphony. It begins with an andante "Prelude" in which nothing is revealed of the sort of dualistic problems that are eventually to take hold of the work; in style and function the movement is more like the first movement of a suite than the opening section of a symphony. Similarly, the very brief, slow first movement of Goehr's *Little Symphony* avoids presenting the basic conflictual antagonisms of the work: it stands dramatically outside the symphony as a kind of prelude or slow introduction to it. The symphony's central dualistic preoccupations appear in the second movement.

A whole group of character shifts—though sometimes slight, and hardly more than an accretion—are a consequence of various stylistic importations by the symphony. This observes an honourable tradition: the symphony has always been open to influences, and indeed it came into being by "democratically" admitting and then attempting to integrate elements from diverse sources. Thus twentieth-century composers have imported the march into the symphonic first movement. Notable examples are the *Trauermarsch* in Mahler's Fifth (the rondo-shaped first part of the multiple first movement), and the sonata-form opening movement of Mahler's Sixth— perhaps among the first symphonies to make the march explicitly the basis of a symphonic first movement. But a march-style need not take over the entire first movement. In Prokofiev's Sixth Symphony a march appears only in the development, where it produces melodic lines that are distinctive and original enough to warrant our regarding them as new thematic material. Such ready and explicit instances represent a distinct development beyond the nineteenth century. This is not true of march slow movements, however (e.g. the second movement of Mahler's Seventh Symphony), for these were already common during the nineteenth century.

The march-scherzo (with its earliest precedent, we recall, in Berlioz) was certainly a rare genre before our century, and appears on limited evidence to have remained so. A fully fledged *alla marcia* scherzo, in orthodox form, is the second movement of Vaughan Williams's Eighth Symphony; Ives, in his Third Symphony, incorporates the march into the scherzo by writing a march-like trio. Other stylistic tendencies of the scherzo are less remarkable: the assimilation of the waltz (Prokofiev's Seventh Symphony, for instance) first hit upon by Berlioz; a free reinterpretation of the dance suite (Stravinsky's Symphony in C); and, merely because we can hardly omit to mention it, the familiar use of the *Ländler* (Mahler). Just as the scherzo has a range of stylistic options, so also there are further possibilities for the other movements: fantasia, cavatina, and toccata (in the first, third, and fourth movements of Vaughan Williams's Eighth Symphony); in the slow movement of the Symphony in C, the style and form of a *da capo* aria, in which Stravinsky's already ornamented, Italianate, and lyrical first section has a still more embellished reprise. Or the integration of hymn tunes, or secular song melodies: the first movement of Copland's Third Symphony, for example, has a hymnic character. More explicitly, in Ives's Third Symphony, the second subject of the first movement is based on the hymn-tune, "O, what a friend we have in Jesus", while the thematic material of the last derives in part from another hymn, "Just as I am without one plea". These and other hymn or secular-song derivations are wholly absorbed into the "musical consciousness" of the symphony, so that they do nothing to hinder its total thematic unity. Better yet, Ives's next symphony, the Fourth, is *founded* upon hymn and song tunes, which it deploys in a complex and always symphonically purposeful way. It draws from the following melodies, among others: Lowell Mason's "Bethany" and "Watchman", Sullivan's "Proprior Deo", "In the Sweet By-and-By", "Yankee Doodle", "Marching through Georgia", "Turkey in the Straw", "Long, Long Ago", "Reveille", "The Irish Fisherwoman", three-ring circus idioms, "Martyn", Oliver Holden's "Coronation", "I Hear Thy Welcome Voice", "Antioch", Woodbury's "Dorrnance", Zeuner's "Missionary Chant", "As Freshmen first we came to Yale", "St. Hilda", and even the "Westminster Chimes"! A closely related procedure is the assimilation of the chorale, a genre claimed for the symphony most emphatically by Bruckner, and cropping up in such twentieth-century pieces as Goehr's *Little Symphony* (first movement), and Honegger's *Symphonie pour Orchestre à Cordes*, where it appears in the coda to the finale as the thematic apotheosis anticipated and searched for during the symphony.

Next among the stylistic imports into the symphony are those deriving from contrapuntal styles and techniques. Here the passacaglia is prominent, and appears to be favoured for use in those movements which are traditionally freest with respect to structure and style— namely, slow movement and finale. Tippett's First Symphony has such a slow movement, and one that aims at a clear differentiation between the ostinato ground, and the subject that expands and proliferates above it. In Shostakovich's Eighth Symphony, a large passacaglia follows on without a break from the second of the two movements that constitute its multiple scherzo. And it creates the strongest possible contrast to the symmetry, extroversion, and preoccupation with physical rhythm, of the two preceding movements. It reaches to great depths of introspection: in its use of contrapuntal passacaglia technique and melisma the movement achieves a freedom from concerns of time and symmetry, and a suspension in the stillness of meditation. In the *Symphonie pour Orchestre à Cordes*, by Honegger, passacaglia technique is adapted to use in an extended ternary slow movement. It provides only the first section—which one might perhaps just as well describe as an unusual form of round, since each division of the eight-bar polyphonic ground repeats the *entire* text of the preceding one. When used in a symphonic finale, passacaglia is a technique that—as Brahms demonstrated in his Fourth Symphony—makes for a powerful sense of monism. This is certainly its effect in the finale of Vaughan Williams's Fifth Symphony, and of Britten's Cello Symphony.

Another contrapuntal style adopted by the symphony is one we have already discussed in a different context, and which will therefore only be touched on now: namely fugue. The final movements of the Sixth Symphony by Hartmann and the First by Walton were mentioned in connection with fugue. Among slow movements, the adagio of Nielsen's Sixth (called "Proposta seria") has a fugato character in each section of its expanded ternary structure, while in Ives's Fourth the slow movement is a conspicuously academic fugue. And the largo of Ives's Third Symphony, though not specifically fugal, is a polyphonic, or (in Tovey's term) "textural" movement, from which dualism has been banished: it is a single, unbroken, unchallenged monistic urge—apt for a movement which also happens to be the finale. There is a fugal scherzo in Nielsen's Fifth Symphony, in addition to other polyphonic sections.

A further group of changes is best described as changes in function: it is this functional difference that seems to be primary, though stylistic modifications may also be involved. Among these is a change in the symphonic role of the scherzo. During the nineteenth century the scherzo grew into a movement of weight and substance—at least, composers came to have the option of treating it as such. But it would be difficult to argue that it came to hold the position of importance that has devolved upon it in some twentieth-century symphonies: namely, a—or perhaps *the*—crucial and decisive stage in the dramatic unravelling of the symphony's central concern: the turning-point that makes possible the finale as the "solution" to the dualistic "problem" that has preoccupied the symphony.[3] Perhaps the first work to give its scherzo that kind of importance is Mahler's Fifth Symphony, where the movement is a huge and complex construction occupying the centre position in the symphony and shouldering a substantial proportion of its emotional and intellectual weight. It is unusual on three principal and related counts. In addition to its being the dramatic turning point of the symphony, it is slightly the longest of the movements and is (as we saw earlier) a formally complex superimposition of a sonata structure and a scherzo with two trios. Its special importance in the work is emphasised by Mahler's calling it Part II: it is the only one of the three parts to consist of a single movement. After the tremendous achievement (in all senses) of the scherzo, there is little left for the two final movements (Part III) to do but bring the work to a close.

Comparable to this is the role of the scherzo in Mahler's Ninth Symphony: there the passage of the music from a condition of growing hysteria mingled with brutality, to one of calm and acceptance in the face of the inevitable, is entrusted wholly to the "*Rondo Burlesque*"—the second part of what we earlier called a multiple scherzo. It is the third of the four movements. The second movement, through a *Ländler* idiom, tried to recover a "world" whose disappearance was a cause of crisis as early as the first movement; but as the attempt began to prove impossible it brought forth bitterness, distortion, and (with the "*Rondo Burlesque*") a savage mockery. Yet in this third movement there is a premonition of a challenge, fully to be realized only in the finale. This occurs in the important section where D Major is attained and held for a period without opposition— the first time this has happened since the end of the opening movement. The dramatic and symbolic import of this episode is plain; it looks back to the tonal attainment of the first movement, and forward to the thematic achievement of the finale. It is the turning-point of the symphony, and in a sense makes possible the spiritual strength of the final movement. Still another example is the scherzo third movement of Elgar's Second Symphony. The movement has an agitation beneath the surface, subliminally as it were; its achievement seems to be that at the heart of the movement (cue 119)—the climax of its sonata-rondo development—it brings to the surface the hidden factor that had apparently accounted for its tonal restlessness, frantic rhythms, and melodic shiftiness. This turns out to be the very same troubling presence that was discovered in the development of the first movement (at cue 28); and its vital relationship to the scherzo is revealed when a superimposition of the principal scherzo motive on the "exposed" melody discloses points of correspondence (scherzo, cue 121). This clarification, this effort of the scherzo, provides the foundation for the affirmative mood of the finale.

A functional change perhaps more easily noticeable than the one we have been discussing concerns the role of the symphonic "conclusion", whether that be coda or finale. The modification here appears to have been almost exclusively—or at least very largely—the prerogative of Vaughan Williams; and so unmistakable is the change that the new descriptive term "epilogue" was invoked by the composer to cope with it. Though on the whole Vaughan Williams's symphonies before the Fourth are at best "fringe" works in terms of the symphonic tradition, that by no means disqualifies them from containing the seeds of the epilogue idea.

The First, the oratorio-like *Sea Symphony*, has a finale that is conventional insofar as it is the climax and goal of the piece. But there are already some unexpected features: being in E flat when the first movement was in D, and being (textually) allegorical when the other movements were fundamentally descriptive, it stands a little outside the main body of the work, and in that sense anticipates Vaughan Williams's characteristic later "amendment" to the symphonic conclusion. The epilogue in the Second (*London*) Symphony is the first to be so-called. It occurs as a long coda-like section after the *Bogen*-form finale, brings with it a change of tone, tempo (andante), and mode (to the minor), and involves a recollection of the introduction to the first movement. It tends toward the condition of the composer's ideal epilogues where, to paraphrase Hugh Ottaway, the entire drama is placed within the still moment of contemplation, and the final perspective of the work is established. The Fifth and Sixth Symphonies provide examples of fully fledged but dissimilar epilogues. In the finale of the Fifth, the process of melodic evolution leads back, near the end (after cue 13), to the point where the symphony began. But if the end is the same as the beginning is the original dualism inescapable? Must the cycle now repeat itself? The suggestion seems to be so. Only the coda, or more appropriately the epilogue, visionary and transcendental, offers a resolution that will ultimately be unchallenged and of permanent stability. It provides the last word, the final perspective; but it is a solution that lies outside the symphony's repeating cycle, belonging no more to its field of action than does an epilogue to a drama.

The extraordinary last movement of the Sixth Symphony is perhaps the finest example of an epilogue. As a slow final movement it is in the tradition of the finale to Mahler's Third and Ninth symphonies, or Tchaikovsky's Sixth— though in the end the comparison only serves to prove its own utter uniqueness. As a finale it is orthodox in that it brings together earlier elements and offers a summing-up: Cooke has shown that "all the vital elements of the first three movements are here gathered together into one theme".[4] And if it is a finale without triumph, it is also a finale without failure. It is the goal not in the usual sense that it has been worked towards, but only in that it is inevitable. It is the final perspective on the drama, but from a point totally outside it and untouched by it. In its other-worldliness it is empty of human emotion: considerations of time and place, here and now, harmony or struggle are irrelevant to its pure, tensionless fugal monism.

Apart from Vaughan Williams, a clear instance of an epilogue is to be found in the *Symphonie Liturgique* by Honegger. There the finale is a sonata form without re-capitulation: the climax of the development, precipitated by the violent sonata conflict, yields instead what can correctly be described only as an epilogue. It lies wholly beyond the domain of the preceding drama: a slow hymn-like section, it is more a vision of transcendental peace than a Beethovenian achievement through conflict. Though certainly integrated thematically, it nevertheless introduces a new hymnic line; and its relinquishment of the original tonal centre is consistent with the symphony's preferred "new-worldly" solution: the epilogue, indeed, seems to give content to the "Dona nobis pacem" of the movement's title.

VI

Early in this chapter we investigated some approaches to the problem of form, posed for the symphony by the breakdown of tonality as the bearer of structure. But if the undermining of the ancient architectonic function of key created problems, it also freed key for a new function: more explicitly than ever before, tonality could now enter into the symphonic drama to play a *symbolic* role. The symphonic composers in the twentieth century who make greatest use of this new potentiality are Mahler and Nielsen. But it is pertinent to note that the use of key symbolism which we continually find in these composers (some critics, referring roughly to the same phenomenon, have called it, less helpfully, "progressive tonality") was not strictly an invention of our century: tonalities have arguably always had some symbolic associations, and in the history of the symphony the attribution of a precise symbolic force to a particular key is as old as Beethoven—though not many symphonists have made use of it. In Beethoven's Ninth Symphony, for instance, the D major of the finale is strikingly hinted at by the blissful second theme of the slow movement and by the exalted trio. Here the successive appearances of D major have broad associations in common, and D major comes to be seen as a goal tonality of the symphony. The same is true of Schumann's Fourth Symphony, where the symbolic tonality is also D major. In Tchaikovsky's Sixth Symphony the recurrent use of two "mood-key" complexes throughout the work (see Chapter 1, page 57) is an extension of the same principle. Wagner was perhaps the first to reckon the use of key as symbol as highly as the use of key as a means of structure and articulation, and Mahler was the first to do so consistently within the symphony. As soon as the use of key as structure is no longer paramount there is no reason why a piece, or a movement, should end in the key in which it began—and in Wagner and Mahler it frequently does not.

Key symbolism is present in Mahler from as early as the First Symphony. An immensely significant and memorable moment in the first movement is the single, brief suggestion of conflict: near the end of the development (about cue 22) the music bristles in apprehension of some lurking danger as snarling, muted brass momentarily undermine the otherwise undisturbed pastoral mood (the movement was originally titled "Spring Without End"). The consequences of this moment are to be felt and explored in the finale, where the gentle second subject in D flat major is unequivocally opposed by the violent first subject, in the non-home key of F minor. Now this first subject derives not only thematically from that one troubled moment in the opening movement, but tonally as well since that passage was *also in F minor*:

EX. 1

This suggests a cyclic—or perhaps more correctly, a leitmotiv—technique, together with a use of key symbolism.

Mahler's symphonies are replete with such instances, where key is vested with a symbolic significance. A few might be singled out. In the slow movement of the Fourth Symphony, a climax is reached where the music shifts suddenly to a celestial E major, the submediant of G major, the main key of both movement and symphony. In the finale there is a related shift: G gives way to E major for the penultimate song stanza, beginning

Kein' Musik ist ja nicht auf Erden,
Die uns'rer verglichen kann werden.
(There is no music on earth to be compared with ours.)

The tonal-symbolic underpinning is unmistakable. In the Fifth Symphony, the A minor second movement introduces at a late stage a new, exultant chorale-like theme in D major. This theme, slightly transformed, returns in the finale where it features as one of the most important subjects; the finale, moreover, is also in D major, and shares a strong affective affinity with the radiant D major section in the second movement. Again, the scherzo (movement three) is in a D major that takes its cue from that same section in the foregoing movement. The Seventh Symphony has a tendency to strive for brightness, to move, so to speak out of the darkness into the light: on a macrocosmic scale this urge is symbolized in the way the symphony lifts itself from a B minor beginning to a conclusion in a brilliant C major—a key that thus appears as a goal tonality. In the first movement C major significantly belongs to the second group, passionately lyrical and standing in real antithesis to the severe, declamatory first group. On a microcosmic scale the striving is suggested in the first of the *Nachtmusik* movements where the principal motive equivocates between major and minor forms of C—the movement is in C *minor*—and has a way of "straightening out" the flattened sixth:

EX. 2

OR:

OR:

There are convincing examples of key symbolism elsewhere than in Mahler (or Nielsen). Vaughan Williams's Eighth Symphony, for example, has a goal tonality of D major which prevails—for but the second time in the entire work—in the last movement: here the recently separated wind and strong bands are reunited and the host of percussion instruments exult in the union. The only other prominent appearance of D major was during the restatement in the first movement, where the music grew affirmatively into a glorious *largamente*. This passage is a varied return of an early *andante sostenuto* section in C major, which stands in dramatic contrast to its diabolical surrounds. C major is thus perceived as being "on the way" to D major: significantly C *minor* is associated with some of the disruptive sections of the first movement. C minor is also the tonality of the scherzo, a slick, jaunty movement, rich in pithy, facile tunes, pungent harmonies, cliché syncopations, even "oom-pah" accompaniment. It is glibly confident music, offering a kind of affirmation different from that arrived at in the first movement: it is the easy alternative, the path of least resistance. Sibelius's Second Symphony swings constantly around the tonal poles of D and F sharp, in their major, minor and aeolian modalities— a means of integration as well as a symbolization. Martinů's Fifth Symphony ends in D, a compromise between— because half-way between—B flat, the work's principal tonal centre, and F, its dominant and important subsidiary in the work: the key of D would therefore seem to be symbolic of the symphony's achieved conciliation of contradictory entities.

In such instances, the symbolic use of key adds a new level of meaning to the music. It contributes: we cannot say that it is fundamental. But with Nielsen's use of the technique we certainly can. In Nielsen's symphonies, key symbolism is essential to the dualistic process: so much is it the very fabric of his symphonic thought that it amounts to the invention of a new kind of musical dialectic. We need to deal with it as such, and must therefore postpone discussion to a later chapter.

NOTES

[1] The work is subtitled "A Symphony for tenor, contralto (or baritone), and orchestra".

[2] This is fully discussed, in a more appropriate context, in Chapter 4.

[3] Beethoven's Pastoral Symphony is a near anticipation; but there the decisive turning-point, the "storm" is treated as a new movement interpolated into an otherwise conventional scheme.

[4] Cooke, Deryck; *The Language of Music*, London 1959, p. 267.

3
Radical structural innovation in the Symphony

I

In the previous chapter we considered aspects of symphonic practice that, even when they seemed particularly novel or surprising, could be related without much difficulty to traditional symphonic procedures. We described these as "moderate" developments. We must now begin to move away from such safe ground and to consider features of symphonic composition that tend sometimes to become quite radical, so much so that they may not only threaten to obscure certain features historically associated with the symphony, but may actually annihilate them altogether. Yet no matter how far these developments go, one thing of course still remains constant and fundamental in all the works we shall consider: namely, a concern for dualism and its musical exploration as the essential preoccupation of symphonic composition. How this dualism is obtained may in some cases be new (and if so will concern us at a later stage); but the fact of it is as old as anything we can properly call the symphonic tradition.

II

We have already seen that two or more types of structure may be united within a single movement. A similar type of integration—but one far more radical in its consequences— is the combination of two or more *movements* into a single structural entity. What is implied here is not any longer the simultaneous application of two or more compatible formal principles within the boundaries of a single movement usually of a characteristic type; we are dealing rather with two or more actual movements which have been synthesized in such a way that they at once retain something of their own distinct individual character, and structurally form a new compound. (The allegretto movement of César Franck's D minor Symphony furnishes an early example—see Chapter 1, page 51.) As such this involves but goes beyond an attempt simply to control the symphonic material, and is a method of binding the symphony into a tighter, more cohesive span: it leads ineluctably towards the one-movement symphony.

At its simplest this technique can appear as the attempt to bring together merely the singular *characters* of different movements—not their associated structures as well—and to enable them to meet within the framework of some appropriate form. For instance, Goehr's *Little Symphony* brings together the characteristics of slow movement and quick finale in its final movement: a meditative first section (*quasi recitando, tempo commodo*) is violently opposed by a noisy, emphatic and more rhythmically regular section (*allegro moderato*); these are rotated in what is an extended ternary scheme. One step further along these same lines is the integration of three movement-characters instead of two, such as occurs in the second and final movement of Webern's Symphony Op. 21. Within the convenient framework of a theme and variations, this movement incorporates broad contrasts of such a kind that it seems to contain in itself the intensifying diversities of scherzo, slow movement, and rapid finale.

A subtler way of combining the characteristics of different movements is that demonstrated by Martinů in the second movement of his Fifth Symphony. Here the distinction between slow and fast tempi is to some extent negated—but still implied—so that (in Peter Evans's words), the movement "does duty for slow movement and scherzo".[1] (The Third and Sixth Symphonies of Martinů, by the way, also include composite movements). Martinů's technique is to choose and keep to a metrical norm— 3/4 and ♩ = 69 throughout—and obtain differentiation through consistent subdivisions and aggregations of the basic metrical unit to create figurations of differing rates of movement. This provides him with a quicker and a slower section, which he then deploys as the basic components of a rondo scheme. Thus the first section uses semiquaver figuration; the second uses notes of relatively bigger value and so appears to move more slowly.[2]

But the integration of symphonic movements can become more complicated than this. A composer may choose to preserve for the purposes of synthesis not only the individual character of different movements, but the *structure* of at least one of them as well. Clearest and most impressive among such syntheses are those in which one of the structural elements to have been fused into the compound is a sonata form: perhaps these are so striking because sonata structure is so strongly individualistic—so unambiguous—a form. Now, in such cases the fusion of movements seems most often to hinge upon a special treatment given to the principle of recapitulation; in brief one may say that the reprise is either transformed or postponed, or both.

Sibelius's Third Symphony, for example, fuses its scherzo and finale by writing the former against a background of sonata structure, and making the development yield the kind of transformations that powerfully generate a finale to *replace* a recapitulation. Or to say the same thing in different terms, so profound are the transformations worked by the development upon the physiognomy of the music, that the "recapitulation" is unrecognizable as such. We need also to observe that this integrated finale, when viewed on its own, is set in a fairly straightforward strophic form: the formal simplicity of one of the components is another fairly recurrent feature of such syntheses, evidently because it avoids an over-complexity of the final structure. Very similar is the first part of Nielsen's Fifth Symphony; a "compound" structure containing two movements in synthesis. Exposition and development (*tempo giusto*) give way not to a restatement but spontaneously to an adagio; thus do first movement and slow movement fuse into a structural unity. The clarity and strength of this structure owes something to the fact that the adagio is a "texture" rather a "shape" movement, to speak in Tovey's terms; it evolves freely and polyphonically according to the dictates of its lines, without an obtrusive form of its own, without even recapitulation.

In these cases, then, a new movement substitutes for recapitulation in the sonata form. A more complex solution is to postpone recapitulation, not replace it; the new movement is then integrated into the music between the end of the development and the recapitulation. A brilliant and complex example is provided by that master of synthesis, Sibelius, in the first part of his Fifth Symphony. If we are to make sense of it, we shall need to discuss this great compound movement more than cursorily. During the development, the processes of dissolution and disintegration are carried far. Eventually there is an enthusiastic recovery, as the development yields eight bars that appear to hint at a kind of recapitulation—though in B major instead of the tonic E flat. But no recapitulation follows. At the ninth bar the change of tempo (to allegro moderato) and metre (from 12/8 to 3/4) simply sounds part of the music's growing excitement at its recovery; germinal growth and thematic transformation inform this music so deeply that this moment—which we shall have to understand as the merging of the first movement with the scherzo—passes smoothly and inevitably.

This scherzo—though it is not so called—is a movement in its own right, as was the first movement. It is set roughly in sonata form: the relative formal complexity of both elements in the compound movement largely accounts for the structural intricacy of the synthesis. Before long E flat is again attained, but the second subject (or generically the trio theme), announced on the trumpets, heralds and is the agent of the collapse back to B: here the scherzo is plunged into development. Two important features are now to be noted. The present second subject soon declares its association with both the subjects of the first movement, and (as Parmet has observed)[3] the *lugubre* bassoon motive from the first movement's development (after cue K)—obviously derived from the accompaniment to the second subject—has penetrated deep into the harmonic structure of this development.

The two movements are thus seen to be in a state of profound interpenetration.[4] What this means is that in a sense this scherzo development is just an extension of the first movement's development—that the two movements are really one and that the development is continuous. Hence the form of this great section operates at one level as an independent first movement with an independent scherzo, and at a higher level as the synthesis of these two to form a single, unified opening movement. But to return to the scherzo's development section: the principal motive— the horn figure from the very beginning of the symphony— is sounded at the original pitch and on the trumpets (after cue N): it is a call to order, and before long a full recovery takes place. This recovery is a recapitulation in that it is an E flat apotheosis of the principal motive, which sounds through majestically on the trumpets and has been absorbed not only into the ostinato accompaniment but into the harmonic texture as well. Here then is a quintessential recapitulation, functioning with respect to the first movement, the scherzo, and the two seen as a single entity.

Almost as complex, but in a different way, is the second part of Nielsen's Fifth Symphony. Here again is a compound structure deploying sonata form with a postponed recapitulation; now, however, *two* movements are sandwiched between development and reprise. Since both of these movements are fugal, and to that extent formally "simple", the ingenious intricacy of Sibelius's compound is not called for. But a special interest of this synthesis derives from the nature of the two newly assimilated movements: they are a scherzo and a slow movement, so that the compound as a whole contains a model of an orthodox four-movement symphonic layout: a sonata-form first movement (minus recapitulation), a scherzo, a slow movement, and a sonata-form finale (i.e. a re-exposition of the original material with some fresh development but without local reprise). The following diagram may help to clarify the special ambivalence of this "bi-structure", as we may conveniently call it:

FOUR-MOVEMENT SYMPHONY	COMPOUND SONATA MOVEMENT
First movement	Exposition
	Development inter-
Scherzo	polations: scherzo
Slow movement	slow movement
Finale	Recapitulation

Nielsen: Fifth Symphony, second part

And here indeed we have the paradigm of many a symphony in one movement. This is not the only type of one-movement symphony, but Nielsen's bi-structural model perhaps provides the clearest illustration of the way in which a one-movement symphony may be related to a tendency towards integration. Let us therefore turn next to the one-movement symphony.

III

We begin, of course, with the sonata bi-structure—a formal type we shall have to recognize as a twentieth-century exfoliation from a very few nineteenth-century experiments in the same direction, perhaps only one of which (Liszt's B minor Sonata) was wholly successful and managed to avoid the pitfalls of "free fantasia". One technique is basic to all our examples of bi-structural "one-movement" symphonies: the recapitulation of the first movement is postponed to the end of the work where it acts as the finale. This much is in common with the syntheses we were last discussing. But one thing is different: and that is that since these bi-structural symphonies are complete works using the old multi-movement principle in an integrated fashion, they must be dealt with primarily from this point of view and only secondarily as instances of expanded first-movement form. A particularly fine example of a bi-structural "one-movement" symphony is Schoenberg's Chamber Symphony Op. 9. Here the superimposition of the conventional four-movement form onto a first-movement structure, so as to create an un-broken and tightly unified multi-movement work, is only one aspect of this symphony's re-thinking of the old symphonic formula.

The first movement, in a standard 4/4 metre, fuses exposition and development into a single entity (a pro-cedure referred to in the previous chapter). Between the first and second subjects is a transition, and after the second subject is a closing section. Normally the development would now follow; but as it has already taken place—through fusion with the exposition—there is instead a suggestion of recapitulation, in the tonic (cue 32). It is certainly only a reminder: nothing more than the first group is referred to. (Properly speaking, recapitulation is deferred.)

The rapid scherzo is mainly in an orthodox triple metre; it contains a contrasting, faster trio in duple time, combines the transition back to the scherzo with a development, and then recapitulates the scherzo—as a counterpoint the trio theme as well—in ten bars. The coda acts also as a transition to the next movement, the main development section of the symphony. Though an interpolation in the present four-movement context, this development is the towering central structure of the piece and brings the symphony to a highly dramatic climax; here, perhaps more than in any other single aspect of the work, the piece reveals its Classical genesis, as Classical techniques are used to spin the section's complex polyphonic web.

The slow movement ensues, and is followed by the finale (cue 90), which uses as its material themes of previous movements. It begins with a transitional theme from the bridge between the first and second subjects in the first division; first- and second-subject ideas return, as do other themes, in a free recapitulation-cum-finale where they are further developed and where their juxtapositions are fresh and revealing. By so drawing together the diverse and contrasting strands of the symphony the finale achieves orthodox conciliation and a sense of fulfilment and purpose.

We have explained the work in terms of the traditional multi-movement form; an account of it in terms of the first-movement form that it involves in synthesis with the other would briefly be as follows: a full exposition and closing section leads by way of an extended interpolation or transition (which we have called the scherzo) to the development; this leads, again by way of an extended interpolation or transition (which we have called the slow movement), to the recapitulation. An interesting feature of the recapitulation is that the themes are not recalled in their original order: the other themes are shown before the arrival of the main theme. The brief coda is common to both formal views of the work—i.e. to the multi-movement symphony and to the sonata structure. We may express this bi-structure diagrammatically:

FOUR-MOVEMENT SYMPHONY	COMPOUND SONATA MOVEMENT
First movement	Exposition
Scherzo	transition (interpolation)
interpolation	Development
Slow movement	transition (interpolation)
Finale	Recapitulation

Schoenberg: Chamber Symphony Op.9.

Schoenberg's Chamber Symphony is a model of bi-structural synthesis and strength. Each formal principle enters equally into the final product, giving and taking in just proportions throughout its length: this explains the appearance of a symmetrical "interlacing" of the two forms in the diagram. It is worth looking briefly at three other bi-structural solutions, each successful in its own different way, but none of them finding the strong mutual integration of the Schoenberg work.

Franz Schmidt's Fourth Symphony is simplest, because closest to a mere linking of four successive movements; its impact as a one-movement symphony depends to a considerable extent on its use of a cyclicism of themes and keys.

FOUR-MOVEMENT SYMPHONY	COMPOUND SONATA MOVEMENT
First movement	Exposition
	Development
Slow movement	interpolations
Scherzo	
Finale	Recapitulation

Schmidt: Fourth Symphony

Robert Simpson's First Symphony has three integrated movements instead of four; the scherzo is absent. It has a formal tautness and unity that derives, again, partly from the fact that the work uses recognizably the same material throughout, and partly from the way the huge development in the sonata form swallows the different movements by stretching itself across most of the work's length.

THREE-MOVEMENT SYMPHONY	COMPOUND SONATA FORM
First movement	Exposition
	Development
Slow movement	
Finale	Recapitulation

Simpson: First Symphony

In the Schmidt and Simpson symphonies, the first movement of the multi-movement symphony was understood as such without difficulty because it was exactly equivalent to the exposition and development of the compound sonata movement. Schoenberg's symphony had no such equivalence; nor does our final example, the Symphony in One Movement by Robin Orr. How then are the first movements of these works understood *qua* first movement? In the Schoenberg this understanding is made possible because the first movement does at least correspond to the compound sonata movement's thematic exposition, and because it contains constant internal development: as far as the first movement is concerned, one would say that exposition and development are concurrent. In the Orr work there is even less correspondence: the first movement of the one structure is equivalent to nothing more than the introduction and first subject of the other. Yet one has no difficulty understanding the first movement as such. One hears it as an "unusual" movement which expands in late-Sibelian fashion from its germinal beginnings, evolves new motifs and is developed according to its own inner dictates and without recourse to any preconceived ground plan—but with a brief sub-dominant recollection of the introduction as a token recapitulation. None of the four movements of the multi-movement structure is conventionally shaped: they are unobtrusive "free" forms. The third movement, moreover, defies expectations on grounds of style. The longest movement in the work, it does not conform to any traditional third-movement type. This is of course accounted for by the fact that it is the compound sonata movement's development section, but is perhaps never-theless a disadvantage if we are looking for a high degree of compatibility between the two inherent structures.

FOUR-MOVEMENT SYMPHONY	COMPOUND SONATA MOVEMENT
First movement	Introduction and first subject
Slow movement	Second subject
Uncharacteristic third movement? or interpolation?	Development
Finale	Recapitulation

Orr: Symphony in One Movement

Our examination of the bi-structural one-movement symphony grew logically out of a discussion of the combination or integration of movements. As such, it has carried this discussion to an extreme point, and we shall not for the moment have any more to say about movement combinations. But we have at the same time been launched upon another inquiry; namely, into the one-movement symphony—and it is this that we need still to pursue a little further.

Not all one-movement symphonies are of the bi-structural type. A single-span symphony could, for instance, retain characteristics of the usual four discrete movements without any parallel reference to a sonata form with postponed recapitulation. The most famous work of this type is the Seventh Symphony by Sibelius. And it is indeed a single indivisible movement: so far have the processes of unification gone that the old multi-movement sectionality is not easily discernable in the synthesis (as it was, say, in Schumann's Fourth Symphony). But there are vestiges of the old pattern. The opening adagio recalls the tradition of the slow introduction, and is furthermore analagous to the traditional first movement in that it is expositional and includes a kind of development after cue D. This gives way to a vivacissimo that is a vestigial scherzo; and the brief ensuing adagio resembles the usual slow movement. Further development leads into what we may call the finale: it is an *allegro molto moderato*, and it resolves the symphony's conflict by deploying the opposites in a fully worked-out sonata form. Then there is an adagio coda.

Now this Sibelius symphony is like all the other single-span symphonies we have seen in that beneath its radical external shape (a *one*-movement symphony) there lurks some form of the traditional structural organization. However, in this work the traditional element is often hardly more than a vestige; and from here it is only a small step to a one-movement symphony that renounces altogether traditional symphonic form. This step has been taken very successfully by Roy Harris, whose Third and Seventh Symphonies, for instance, are each in one unbroken movement that conserves nothing of the old formal schemes.

The Third Symphony is a "textural" movement without any compromise with "shape": its principle is one of perpetual evolution, in which everything springs from the opening, and grows continually through a technique of linear evolution and permutation. During this process different stages are passed through, which contrast with others; but they are incidental and transient, merely the result of what came before and the progenitors of what is to follow, and in no sense opposed to each other. And these stages do not mean that the work is governed by considerations of "shape": to speak of "sections" is merely to observe the various phases through which the work in its organic development passes: it is impossible here to speak meaningfully of a "ground-plan". What appears to be recapitulation is in fact in a sonata sense not so, at least not more so than a fugal stretto is a "recapitulation": it is merely a recrudescence of former features, not conveying a sense of reprise, but partaking in and essential to this further, and unbroken, development.

Commentators who speak of a "ground-plan" here, or imply a "shape", have been misled by such characteristics, as well as by the swiftness of some of the mutations and metamorphoses, which results in a superficial formal sectionality. The swift changes, however, are due to an extreme compression in some of the stages of metamorphosis, or even an elision of "links". Each new "section" is precipitated by a crisis, by a moment of heightened excitement, great activity, and tension: it is in such moments of enhanced mental and emotional sensibility that sudden abrupt transitions are made. These metamorphoses have a visionary quality in their un-expectedness but seeming "rightness" and inevitability, and they give to the evolving thematic network a sense of sudden elision or of compression of links in the chain.

The composer's satisfactory summary of the resultant stages or "sections" of the work is given below. The big crises, causing significant metamorphoses, occur between the major divisions, while the lesser crises, which give rise to correspondingly smaller transformations, occur between the "sub-sections".

Section I   Tragic—low string sonorities.
Section II   Lyric—strings, horns, woodwinds.
Section III   Pastoral—woodwinds with a polytonal string background.
Section IV   Fugue—dramatic.
              A   Brass and percussion predominating.
              B   Canonic development of materials

		from Section II constituting background for further development of fugue.
	C	Brass climax, rhythmic motive derived from fugue subject.
Section V		Dramatic—Tragic.
	A	Restatement of violin theme of Section I; tutti strings in canon with tutti woodwinds against brass and percussion developing rhythmic idea from climax of Section IV.
	B	Sections I and IV over pedal timpani.

It must be stressed again that this is not a "shape", any more than a fugue is a "shape"; it is a "texture", and the composer's summary and division into "sections" is merely a useful aid to comprehension. The "sections" bear no comparison to the formal sections of a traditional symphony. In such a work sonata duality must necessarily rest on new factors; precisely what these are we shall see in due course.

IV

This chapter began with a discussion of radical combinations of movements—which led us logically into a consideration of the one-movement symphony. This in turn has raised a new issue: the possibility of abandoning traditional symphonic organization, either to a very large degree (Sibelius's Seventh) or indeed completely (Harris's Third and Seventh). Once symphonic composers make some radical break with traditional form, the options for new types of structure would seem to be limitless. Yet paradoxically, more often than not these new forms come to life within a three- or four-movement layout whose individual movements have outward aspects of *character* and *function* that bear a marked similarity to those of traditional symphonic movements. In such works there is usually a first movement, probably fast, that broaches the main business of the symphony, a slow movement, a scherzo-type movement, and a finale which brings resolution; or one of the middle movements is omitted.

Now it is within this rough external schema that many of the interesting formal innovations occur; and the bulk of the ensuing discussion will therefore concern a variety of such innovations, ranging from the less to the more radical. Since works that have a radical structure in one movement tend to have another such structure in a different movement, we shall find a fairly large number of highly innovatory movements within a much smaller number of symphonies. From many points of view it will be useful to confine our examples to one such small group of works. I propose, then, to draw from the following symphonies: Tippett's Second, Martinů's Fourth and Fifth, Goehr's *Little Symphony*, Shostakovich's Fourth, Ives's Fourth, and Gerhard's First.

Our first question is this: in the absence of sonata form, how might the symphonic first movement be structured? One answer is that other, known, forms may be used as alternatives to sonata form, provided they can be reconciled in some way with the demands of symphonic dualism. This has been the approach of Martinů, who has drawn from Baroque and pre-Classical sources. The form of the first movement of his Fourth Symphony exhibits affinities with the eighteenth-century dance suite. It is a binary structure, the two main sections of which are, however, not repeated: the first section ends away from the B flat major home key, and the second begins away from that key but moves back to it: moreover, the second section expands the material of the first but follows closely its contours, so that the formal result is an asymmetrical binary in which the second section has approximately 122 bars to the 88 of the first. Further, the second section's handling, or quasi-development, of the material of the first (for instance after cue 8 or between cues 10 and 12) adumbrates sonata development and sonata form in a sense that also has historical precedence in the dance suite. Apart from these main formal divisions each section is further subdivisible into two segments, distinguished partly by a tempo change. The whole movement may therefore be represented diagrammatically as follows:

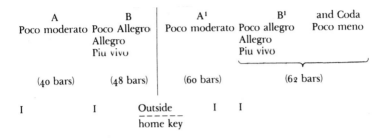

A	B		A¹	B¹	and Coda
Poco moderato	Poco Allegro		Poco moderato	Poco allegro	Poco meno
	Allegro			Allegro	
	Piu vivo			Piu vivo	
(40 bars)	(48 bars)		(60 bars)	(62 bars)	
I	I	Outside	I	I	
		home key			

On the crucial question of dualism, the point is that the work moves from kinds of organization, style, and interest in non-dualistic contrast that might loosely and generally be called "Baroque", through a process of clarification and sharpening of contrasts, to kinds of organization, style, and concern with dualism that obviously have traditionally symphonic connections. This "progress" is in fact only a shift of emphasis: there are clearly aspects of each in the other. Martinů's own analysis of the symphony observes that the first movement is based on "two short one-bar elements (cellules) and upon the difference between the lyrical element and rhythmic semi-quaver movement"[1]:

EX. 3

and draws attention to the fact that they are introduced and deployed "without any special tension". But the difference between them, though non-dualistic at first, is at the core of the symphony: it is the way these two broadly differentiated elements *interact upon each other and change each other*—though at first non-conflictually—and then ultimately become *sharply drawn opposites in a dualism that stands in need of resolution*, that relates the movement, and finally the work, in an important sense to the conventional symphony.

A work which has the same provenance as Martinů's Fourth Symphony, but which makes a different type of compromise with the sonata principle, is the same composer's Fifth Symphony. Its first movement is equally far from sonata structure: it uses forms and stylistic principles which have their origins in ritornello forms and in the dance suite, but it succeeds in combining these with the symphonic idea of contrasting identities whose relationship—whose mutual conflict—becomes the prime concern of the work. The movement differs from its counterpart in the Fourth Symphony in that it does not begin with incipient identities which are steadily brought to fullness, but rather with mature contrasts. Duality rests upon the differences between the adagio section of the movement and the allegro section, whose varied and frequent alternation defines the ABABA form of the movement. The contrasting tempi are one important feature of this differentiation. But there are others. For instance, the adagio defines itself over-against the allegro by involving the use of *motive* rather than *theme*. The thematic allegro section, indeed, bears a relation to the adagio similar to that borne by a Classical symphonic exposition to its slow introduction. One might perhaps go so far as to say that the adagio here *is* the old slow introduction, but elevated to the status of subject-group and active participant in the drama.

But we are still on familiar ground. By forgoing sonata form and choosing Baroque or pre-Classical form, Martinů has negated one formal convention in order to affirm another. This is not the approach of most composers of formally unorthodox first movements. Tippett's Second Symphony has a formally unique but simple first movement, one written outside of conventional structures but retaining the lucidity of procedure and design of orthodox sonata. The movement is formally conventional to the extent only that it is based on the contrast of two thematic complexes, the first basically in C, steely, rhythmical, and of brittle (mainly string, brass and piano) textures, the second setting out from E flat major, of supple *carillonando* (mainly woodwind) lines, and chastely interwoven counterpoints. Tippett loosely calls the movement a "dramatic sonata allegro"; but decidedly unusual about it is that instead of the traditional plan it has four closely related main sections described by the composer as "statement, first argument, re-statement, second argument and coda". The "arguments" are not normal developments at all, but reviews of the expositional material with some variation, regrouping, and a tendency to derive new shapes from old material. The movement, then, consists of four basically similar—and in length almost exactly equal—presentations of the same material.

Tippett's movement is a marvel of formal lucidity and simplicity. These qualities are certainly unusual among movements which are formally un- or anti-conventional, for the absence of recognizable structures tends to lead rapidly toward formal complexity. But this is not necessarily a bad thing: complexity, after all, brings with it its own potential. A good example of a complex, anti-conventional first movement is provided by Shostakovich's Fourth Symphony. "I am not afraid of difficulties", said the composer while writing this work. "It is perhaps easier, and certainly safer, to follow a beaten path, but it is dull, uninteresting and futile." Certainly his first movement has nothing whatever to do with the beaten path. But if old methods of structural organization—including functionally contrasting tonalities—are discarded in favour of an unpredictable, complex, and more diverse organization, the fundamental symphonic principles remain the same.

The movement rests on the principle of bringing together a series of diverse and highly contrasted materials and exploiting the tension so produced; at the same time the contrasts are subjugated to the whole by being worked into the total texture and interrelated. The movement may be accounted for in the following way (in this analysis each section, indicated by a Roman capital, is an extended paragraph):

A: Militaristic opening. Tutti. C minor. Transition leads to—

B: (Cue 7) C is still the tonal centre. Quieter and more lyrical. Mainly for strings, but some woodwind. Quickens into—"Development", dominated by the harsh rhythms and timbres, the ostinatos, of "A"; not a Classical development but an entrenchment of certain ideas which then proliferate or, alternatively, become the centre of static preoccupations. Tutti. After a climax gives way via a brief link to—

C: (Cue 24) Ambiguous tonality: C, mainly, over an immovable A flat pedal. A Stravinskyan toccata for woodwind. A brief tutti outburst, fierce and dissonant, provides a grimly contrasting backdrop for—

D: (Cue 31) A sparsely orchestrated section, based on a simple and meditative bassoon melody in 3/8 and D minor.
Further "development", tutti and at a high dynamic level, and making conspicuous use of the material of "D".

E: (Cue 51) A "scherzando" section, scored mainly for woodwind and pizzicato strings, in brilliant, gossamer textures. Eventually precipitates—

F: (Cue 63) A relentless presto fugue, centred on F, for strings alone at first, but later for full orchestra. Incorporates figures from previous sections, and uses the fugal subject in varying degrees of augmentation and mutation. Expands to create the huge central climax of the movement. An anticipatory link leads to—

G: (Cue 81) A bitter waltz parody in C sharp minor, creating in its ribald banality and forced gaiety the most violent contrast with the grim preceding section. Its second melody is based on a variation of section "D"—the first of what is to become a quickening cycle of reprises. Mainly strings and bass clarinet. A series of steadily incremental brass-and-percussion crescendos leads to—

RECAPITULATION: (Cue 91) C minor. Extremely free and truncated, so much so that—except for one or two places—it hardly sounds like a recapitulation at all. The recapitulation follows a course based roughly on the following sections and in the following order: "A", "D", "B", "A". The movement ends in C minor.

Attention needs to be called to several points: the clear definition and contrasting character of each section; the way this is supported by the contrasting orchestral "registration" of each; the use of developments (orthodox in this sense at least) to exploit the tensions and contradictions and build the climaxes; the way the developments, in contrast to the principal sections, use the full orchestra; the fact that the only link with orthodox formal procedure is the quasi-recapitulation at the end.

And there are first movements that have even less than this to do with the organizational habits of sonata. Ives's Fourth Symphony has a brief through-composed first movement which is merely a "free" exposition of the basic thematic material of the work and its central concern—both of these inextricably linked to the symbolic and associative possibilities of hymnic and secular tunes. The movement has something of a preludial character—but less so than the first movement of Goehr's *Little Symphony*, a mere nineteen-bar slow chorale scored for strings. And in Gerhard's First Symphony, the first movement depends on the fact that the work uses the total serial field. This means that from the basic twelve-note series are derived correlated proportional sets which control the work in its manifold parameters and which articulate its form in terms of what Gerhard called superordinate time-levels. These levels, or layers, says Gerhard,

open up fan-wise, each articulating itself within its proper range, and contributing (as a whole) to the articulation of the next higher level, where it becomes simply a member of the superordinate structure; and so forth, up to the highest level which is the whole, in the light of which the parts achieve their proper meaning.[6]

In such a work, the form of the first (or any) movement

clearly cannot be understood separately from the serial matrix.

The middle movements of this group of symphonies are less interesting to our current discussion. They stay much closer to traditional structures—with one exception: the second (scherzo) movement of Ives's Fourth Symphony. Certainly this is a movement making use of conflict between themes; but the manner, if not the principle, is quite new, since something like a score of sacred and secular tunes are deployed with a superficial randomness in a form that is thoroughly through-composed. If the movement has no sophisticated tonal or melodic discipline, no organized development, none of the civilized virtues of Classical sonata, it is because, as Mellers has so succinctly put it, Ives

> had behind him the American wilderness, not Viennese civilization and a long musical tradition; so that he cannot accept Beethoven's positives—especially that of eighteenth-century tonality, on which the classical idea of sonata depended.[7]

Where the middle movements were (with this single exception) relatively conservative, the finales tend towards the degree of formal radicalism of the first movements. And they tend, moreover, to be informed by the same innovatory formal principles as their first movements, on occasion even to run parallel to them. By doing twice what seemed strange once, a work may achieve structural coherence and a level of intelligibility that it might otherwise lack. The last movement of Martinů's Fifth Symphony is a very clear instance of a finale using a structure that consciously runs parallel to that of the first movement. Not only is there a similar duality of alternating slow and fast sections, but as in the opening movement the first of these sections is motivic and the second thematic. The way the lento generates the allegro corresponds to the first movement; the first sections of both movements resolve long dominant pedals onto tonic assertions of B flat major; and there is a further obvious parallel between the two movements in the tempo and metre relationships in each:

First movement—adagio, C: allegro, ¢.
Final movement—lento, 3/4: allegro, 6/8.

The overall formal correspondence between this movement and the first may be shown schematically:

I	A	B	A	B	A	
	adagio	allegro	adagio	allegro	adagio	(coda-like)

	A	B	A	B		
III	lento	allegro	lento	allegro	coda	(extension of B)

Taking into account the rondo form of the central movement, the work as a whole reveals an astonishing and radically unconventional symmetry:

$$\xleftarrow{\hspace{3cm}}\mid\xrightarrow{\hspace{4cm}}$$
ABABA/ABACABA/ABAB coda
I   II   III

Martinů's Fifth provides our clearest illustration of what one might call the structural empathy of unconventional outer movements. Tippett's Second Symphony has a finale that does not run parallel to the opening, though its four sections certainly remind one of the four sections of the first movement; Tippett himself has pointed out the connection. The first movement had four cohesive sections (statement, first argument, restatement, second argument); the finale's four sections refer to those of the first movement by using the opposite principle of *dis*connection between them: the first section is "additive" and repetitive (in a way that, incidentally, recalls the third movement), the second is a passacaglia, the third an unfolding melody, and the fourth a repeating *Urthema*. This last section, moreover, recalls not only the main theme of the first movement, but also that very movement's principle of repetition.

In Shostakovich's Fourth Symphony, the first movement was through-composed to seven sections (which we called A, B, C, D, E, F and G) and rounded off with a very free recapitulation; the finale is through-composed to five sections (A, B, C, D, E) plus coda. In Ives's Fourth, the finale is likewise through-composed but, as one might expect, in the manner of its own first (and second) movements:

without "sections". However, this eventually turns into a sort of grand, free recapitulation, not only of this but also of earlier movements.

For all their formal originality, the works we have just been discussing have at least this much structurally in common, and in common also with the symphonic tradition: that they preserve the outer shell of the multi-movement symphony, the logical succession of three or four separate movements with something of their traditional character and function. Innovation can go further than this—as indeed we already know from our study of the one-movement symphony. There we saw that a composer could not only integrate several movements into a single unbroken span, but could also abandon even the vestiges of orthodox symphonic structure and organize the one-movement symphony according to quite "alien" principles. How might the multi-movement symphony take this final step, and abandon even these vestiges? Can one conceive of a true symphony in several movements, where not only the "internal" organization of those movements but *also their "external" succession* breaks radically with symphonic convention? To be sure, such symphonies are a very rare genre. But one that demonstrates with remarkable clarity and conviction how such a thoroughly anti-conventional multi-movement symphony might be structured is Iain Hamilton's Sinfonia for Two Orchestras. So radical is this work's rethinking and recreation of the norms of the symphonic tradition that it also involves a new procedure for incarnating and working out that essential characteristic of symphonic thought, a preoccupation with musical duality. That aspect of the work we shall discuss fully at a more appropriate time; we must now consider mainly its forms.

The Sinfonia consists of eleven short sections, each of which has its own instrumental registration; i.e. each section except those at the beginning and the end is scored either for one of the "orchestras" of the work's title, or for one of the major instrumental "families"; the outer sections of the work are scored for the tutti orchestral ensemble. Those sections written for the "family" groups are called *Tessiture*—appropriately, for they are pre-eminently "textural", and the consistent use of the word calls attention to the similarities and differences between each *Tessitura* on the one hand, and between the *Tessiture* and the orchestral sections on the other. Except for the sections at the beginning and at the end, the *Tessiture* alternate strictly with the orchestral movements. The whole sequence, together with all tempo indications, is as follows:

1.	Le due orchestre	Sostenuto	♩ = 60	4/4
2.	Orchestra I	Allegro molto	♩. = 126	6/8
3.	Tessitura 1	Lento ma non troppo	♩ = 60 (Percussion)	5/4
4.	Orchestra II	Vivace	♩ = 132	4/4
5.	Tessitura 2	Andante	♩ = 60 (Strings)	3/4
6.	Orchestra II	Poco lento	♩. = 38 ♪ = 114	6/8
7.	Tessitura 3	Lento non troppo	♩ = 60 (Brass)	5/4
8.	Orchestra I	Scherzoso	♩ = 132	4/4
9.	Tessitura 4	Lento non troppo	♩ = 60 (Woodwind)	3/4
10.	Le due orchestre	Allegro molto	♩. = 126	6/8
11.	Le due orchestre	Sostenuto	♩ = 60	4/4

The contrast between the *Tessiture* and the orchestral sections—alluded to above—is further emphasised by the contrast between their various time signatures and tempi: the *Tessiture* employ triple and additive metres (3/4, 5/4), and uniform tempi (♩ = 60), while the *Orchestre* use simple and compound duple metres (4/4, 6/8) and widely differing tempi. Moreover, the constantly changing tempi and metres—which are however maintained with unbroken consistency throughout the course of a movement—enhance the contrast between adjacent movements, much as these traits have traditionally enhanced contrasts between adjacent movements in symphonic writing. The form of the work, then, clearly articulates what is one of the basic issues of the work: the exploration of these multiple instrumental conflicts.

The first section calls attention to the symphony's central

dualistic concern; it is thus a kind of exposition. Sections 2 to 10 inclusive may be said to correspond to the traditional development of a symphony: of course they are not development in any orthodox particulars of method or style, but only in that they examine, extend, fully reveal, and clarify the issues inherent in the first section's "exposition". But at the same time these sections function in a way that is very similar to the function of differentiated movements in the traditional symphony—i.e., as em- bodiments of opposing principles, and often as different embodiments of the same principle. Once separated, the opposing orchestras are not united again until Section 10, where the percussion leads the return of all the instruments into the fray. Soon (Section 11) their reunion is celebrated by the full emancipation of the big climactic melody that brings the work to an end. These last two sections act as a traditional symphonic finale; the very last may perhaps be said to operate as a coda as well. The beginning of Section 10, with the percussion instruments entering one by one and then being joined by other instruments in a steadily ascending dynamic, builds an excitement that has a typically "finale" character in its suggestion of imminent fulfilment.

Having remarked on the Sinfonia's re-integration, in principle, of exposition, development, and finale, we may now hope to find other "atavistic" resemblances to traditional forms. And indeed one might point out that in its sostenuto tempo the first section retains a hint of the old slow introduction; that roughly three-quarters of the way through the work—i.e. at a place corresponding to the traditional scherzo—there is a section marked scherzoso; and that the slowest section (No. 6), a poco lento, is placed, as an orthodox slow movement might be, at or near the middle of the work. Moreover, this movement marks the turning point of the work by beginning the reprise in retrograde of the first five movements of the work at their original speed, and, to a large extent, original pitch. The suggestions of recapitulation here are unmistakeable. If the Sinfonia for Two Orchestras amounts to a far-reach- ing reappraisal of one area of the past—the traditional symphony—Hamilton himself has articulated his felt need for such a reappraisal:

> As we no longer consider tonality to be the overriding power it is no longer logical to employ these forms [i.e. sonata, rondo, fugue]. We are concerned with re-appraising basic elements such as variation, texture, density, recapitulation, dynamic, instrumentation, etc.[8]

And elsewhere he has said:

> The evolution of logical forms from asymmetrical concepts is of vital importance. This can only be achieved by continual reappraisal of all the basic elements of any form.[9]

V

Towards the end of the previous chapter we considered a variety of stylistic importations into the symphony from genres and idioms not conventionally associated with symphonic or sonata writing. Our examination was not very extensive: we were dealing exclusively with moderate innovations and looked therefore only at foreign styles that were introduced into the symphony in such a way and to such an extent as not to affect the symphony's own general character. But it is the task of the present chapter to deal with radical developments; and we shall therefore look now at works whose whole character has been affected by the extensive appropriation of a "non-symphonic" style.

We must be brief at first. We have already dealt with two symphonies by Roy Harris—the Third and the Seventh. We saw that these single-span symphonies were "textural" works without any compromise with principles of "shape": this is so because fundamental to these works is the radical importation of a *polyphonic style*. These symphonies are a perpetual evolution; everything in them springs from their openings and evolves continuously through the linear growth of independent contrapuntal lines. Their processes of growth are evolutionary and variational rather than developmental in any orthodox sense. Since they depend on thinking that is linear, lyrical and polyphonic, the movements of their tonal centres are aspects of this growth, dictated by the necessities of line. There is no tonal dialectic as in the traditional symphony: tonal movements are incidental rather than integral and dynamic.

Where the Harris Symphonies radically appropriate polyphony and yet remain essentially concerned with sonata duality, there are other symphonies that effect a profound compromise with *Baroque and pre-Classical styles and forms*: here we must make passing allusion again to the Fourth and Fifth Symphonies of Martinů. We suggested earlier that these works adopted characteristics of the dance suite and ritornello form; and we argued that, despite some resultant unsymphonic aspects, they succeeded in bringing to life a genuine symphonicism.

The Harris and Martinů symphonies are, as we know, highly original structurally, in addition to their being stylistically radical. Indeed, in so far as these works are concerned, the two aspects are inseparable: each depends on the other. But it is not a necessity that extreme structural and stylistic innovation should be linked: our two final examples have largely conventional forms but are stylistically very unconventional through having drawn from idioms outside the symphony. In the Britten Symphony for Cello and Orchestra this importation is from the neighbouring realm of the concerto; it is thus assimilated without difficulty. Here the relationship between the soloist ("the individual") and the orchestra ("the society") differs from that which usually obtains in a concerto: instead of the soloist being in opposition to the orchestra, he is a kind of spokesman *for* the orchestra, leading them, arguing on their behalf. He leads the discussion; he appears at the beginning of the movements—without having to wait for any ritornello—announces the principal themes, and is always the first to offer a definitive new melodic line: the significant exception is in the last movement, a late stage of the drama, where the soloist's role as spokesman has changed. Otherwise it is he who leads, who usually takes the music from one section to another and so creates form for the piece; and it is he who generally speaks most emphatically of all. Significant stages in the development of the relationship between cello and orchestra are the recapitulations of the first and slow movements. The first movement has a fairly strict recapitulation in which the most striking—and meaningful—change is that it is now the orchestra, rather than the solo cello, that handles the main themes: reversing the priorities of the exposition, the cello plays the subsidiary or accompanimental themes. In the recapitulation of the slow movement the cello again relinquishes its former role: it now takes up subsidiary thematic figures. By the time we reach the finale (a passacaglia) the relationship has altered markedly: the finale is the only movement in which an instrument other than the cello introduces a main theme. Of course the cello has a major theme too—the ground. But the roles are now more equal, for, as a result of the symphonic drama and of the cello's efforts in it on behalf of the orchestra, the finale is not only a movement in which the monistic technique of divisions upon a ground can flourish but also a time when the orchestra has been liberated into a group of individuals. The trumpet is the first to claim its new "solo" status: it erupts with the principal theme, while the cello is content to support it with the ground. And this principal theme is the most "open" melody there has so far been in the symphony, the most purely song-like. In this new society all men may speak openly, and no-one has any prior claims to being able to speak first: anybody may become a "soloist": there are tendencies in this movement for instruments to break out of the orchestral texture and temporarily assume solo roles. At cue 69, for instance, the word "solo" appears five times in the score in two bars. The movement drives to its conclusion in a spirit of clear, chorale-like affirmation, with the cello taking its part alongside the other instruments on the melodic line. The achievement is in the broad Beethoven tradition.[10]

Considerably more problematic in principle is the attempt to import song into the symphony. Here there is the enormous difficulty of reconciling the specific quality

of the song texts (and their need for an appropriate setting), with the intrinsically musical demands of symphonic
dualism—opposing demands that simply do not arise when
the symphony adopts something of the concerto style. Now
ever since Beethoven's Ninth Symphony composers have
attempted to enrich the symphony by importing into it
vocal styles—usually operatic: a tendency that culminated
in Wagner's writing of operas in a symphonic style. But it is
arguable that none of the nineteenth-century "vocalized"
symphonies written after Beethoven was genuinely
symphonic. Beethoven's finale achieved true symphonism
because it retained musical (sonata) process as primary, and
invoked the text to make specific and explicit what was
already implicit in the music; the important procedure by
which the Ode theme is arrived at, for example, takes place
without voices, and it is only when this section is *repeated* that
voices are invoked. After Beethoven, this priority was lost
and the text tended to become paramount. Of later
composers, whether in the nineteenth or the twentieth
centuries, it is perhaps only Mahler who achieves a genuine
vocal symphonism. And even then he is not always
successful. But a work of his which is both very radical in its
assimilation of vocal style and extraordinarily successful in
symphonic terms, is *Das Lied von der Erde*. The coincidence of
these two features—its radicalism and its success—makes
the work probably unique in the history of attempts to
integrate voice into the symphony.

The vocal style which *Das Lied* imports into the symphony
is that of the song cycle: the work is subtitled "A symphony
for tenor, contralto (or baritone), and orchestra". From the
very outset it is apparent that purely musical considerations
are allowed to take precedence over the text, which is
therefore not a programmatic tyrant of the inner structure.
The opening movement is clearly a (modified) sonata
structure. The first verse is the exposition, wherein the last
four lines (beginning *Wenn der Kummer naht*) assume second-
group material and substitute D minor for the first group's
opening A minor. The second verse is a varied counter-
exposition. Plainly, the dualism here is purely a matter of
musical organization and logic: the words do not support

any antithesis, but seem on the contrary almost to ride over it. This is not to say that the text does not have any dualistic import or that, if it does, its expression never coincides with that of the musical dualism. As the text unfolds it reveals its own internal oppositions which support, and are supported by, the symphonic antitheses, mainly at the inter-movement level. The music of the third and fourth verses is developmental in the Mahlerian manner, and the brief final verse is a terse recapitulation.

The second movement, "*Der Einsame im Herbst*", contrasts musically with the first, while textually (and let us notice the independence again) it expands the mood of lines from the first verse of that movement:

> *Wenn der Kummer naht,*
> *Liegen wüst die Garten der Seele,*
> *Welkt hin und stirbt die Freude, der Gesang.*

(When care draws near, the garden of the soul
lies waste, and joy—the song—fades and dies.)

At that point the key was D minor: here it is also D minor, a fact that symbolically reinforces the connection. The next three movements, "*Von der Jugend*", "*Von der Schönheit*", and "*Der Trunkene im Frühling*", together constitute a strong contrast to the other movements of the work (textually *as well as* musically). We have already argued (p. 119) that they function as a multiple scherzo.

The finale, "*Der Abschied*", is a setting of two poems, and the longest movement. It begins in C minor and ends in C major, the relative of the opening movement. As in the first movement, musical structure—the autonomy of musical progression—takes precedence over the text; the resultant form begins to look like sonata. The expositional sections entail their own Mahlerian quasi-developments, with fertile proliferations that are freer than normal but still models of consistency. Between the setting of the first text and that of the second there occurs the longest instrumental interlude in the work; this satisfies the triune purpose of giving a wholly orchestral-developmental thrust to the movement, of separating the two texts (for they are different, and though wonderfully wrought by Mahler into mutual interdependence and unity they nevertheless demand a separating interval), and of actively involving us in the protagonist's period of waiting:

Ich stehe hier und harre meines Freundes;
Ich harre sein zum letzen Lebewohl.

(I stand here awaiting my friend; I wait
till his last farewell.)

The second poem (*Er stieg vom Pferd und reichte ihm den Trunk des Abschieds dar ...*) behaves as a recapitulation, freely varied, pliable, and finally transfigured. The point here is that the notion of thematic reprise, which is a purely musical, purely structural thing existing independently of the text, has won. As in the first movement, employment of dualistic sonata form within the movement is, apart from being a means of generating and sustaining a large structure, a method of symphonic control and organization. It makes possible restraint, a strict marshalling of materials, interdependence of parts, total coherence and unity, and the supression of the part in favour of the whole. These are genuinely symphonic considerations.

We have already noted that the contrasts between some of the movements are dramatic. This is the musical expression of the conflict-in-need-of-resolution, mirrored by the agonizing preoccupations of the text. This inter-movement conflict coincides with, and is given precision by, the main concern of the text: a conflict arising from a love of life in the face of approaching death. The duality between, say, "*Von der Jugend*" and "*Der Einsame im Herbst*", is fully inherent in the music itself—and this musical duality gains only in particularity once we know that the texts by their juxtaposition point an antithesis between the weariness and loneliness of one whose *kleine Lampe erlosch mit Knistern*, and the life-force of youth.[11]

NOTES

[1] "Martinů the Symphonist", *Tempo*, 55/56 (1960), p. 26.

[2] Šafránek, Martinů's biographer and critic, has observed this also—though his elucidation is not as clear as it might be—in a passage that calls attention to the deliberateness of the device on the part of the composer:

"A notable feature of the Fifth Symphony is its 'newer, better structure', as the composer himself remarked to me shortly after its completion, adding that it had not the old form of the symphony. 'I have tried to show this structure schematically, but its new motion, especially noticeable in the Larghetto, comes out most clearly on listening to the composition as a whole'. In Martinů's vocabulary, the word 'motion' has the meaning of ordered movement or dynamic order, in which modern poly-rhythmic patterns and rhythmic irregularities give way to an internal dynamic order where bar-lines lose their relevancy and where *the difference between quick and slow tempos is mutually cancelled out*: semiquavers in slow tempo maintain the motion of crotchets in an Allegro. The Larghetto of the symphony is a striking illustration of this new dynamic relationship." (My italics).

In *Bohuslav Martinů: His Life and Works*, p. 250.

[3] Parmet, Simon; *The Symphonies of Sibelius*, p. 75.

[4] It is now evident that these were indeed conceived as separate movements, and were only integrated subsequently. See Robert Layton's statement in the *Musical Times*, August 1968, p. 729.

[5] Written for the first performance of the work on December 11, 1945, in Philadelphia, and reprinted in Šafránek, Milos; *op. cit.*, p. 242 f.

[6] *The Score*, September 1956, p. 70. The whole of the relevant article—"Developments in twelve-tone technique"—should be consulted for a full discussion by the composer of his methods, outlined here.

[7] *Music in a New Found Land*, p. 48.

[8] *Tempo*, No. 55/56, Autumn–Winter 1960.

[9] See Schafer, Murray; *British Composers in Interview*, London 1963, p. 158.

[10] Some of the ideas here governing the relationship between the solo instrument and the orchestra—though used to different dramatic ends—are clearly presaged by Britten's Piano Concerto Op. 13 (especially in the first movement), written some fifteen years earlier, and to some extent also by the Violin Concerto, written a year after the Piano Concerto. See for instance Evans,

Peter; "Sonata Structures in Early Britten", *Tempo*, Autumn 1967, pp. 7–8.

[11] As has been suggested, *Das Lied* is probably unique as a genuine song symphony. And in saying this one is not forgetting Mahler's Eighth Symphony. It is true in only a limited sense that the logic of that work is the logic of the music's own internal drama and that the text exists to give precise meaning to that drama. In Part I the logic is that of the Latin hymn, *Veni creator spiritus*, and in Part II that of the closing scenes of Goethe's *Faust*. The work is a setting of these two pieces, and, but for some respects in which it transcends this definition, might possibly be described as a Romantic cantata. Perhaps this is why the work (it seems to me) has no *significantly* generative musical dualisms. Contrasts tend to be incidental (rather than fundamental) to the structure, to occur within the relatively small limits allowed by each text. In any case it is the affinities, rather than the contrasts, between the various parts of the texts—and between the different texts themselves—that the composer seems bent on exploring. None of this is to deny the work's thematic unity or its important thematic transformations, which give it a preoccupation that exists only in relation to its totality; nor is it, of course, in any sense to argue against the greatness of the work.

Part Three

The Twentieth Century: Innovation in "Content"

4
Symphonic conflict redefined

Our study must now begin to move in a new direction. So far we have been concerned mainly with questions of structure; now we turn to another aspect of the modern symphony, one which we occasionally hinted at in previous chapters but whose discussion we were forced to postpone to a later stage when it could be dealt with fully. This other aspect, which is of vital and fundamental importance in the twentieth-century symphony, is the invention or development of new methods for incarnating symphonic dualism. There are several such methods; in the present chapter we shall investigate the one which seems to be the most widespread, and is therefore perhaps the most important.

We saw in Chapter 1 that the dualism of the Classical symphony depended on the contrast of objective themes and/or tonalities, and that this means of duality, which was also the basis of the subsequent reconciliation, was made possible partly by the structural capabilities of a complete system of tonality. We saw also that the dualistic principle was soon associated specifically with the notion of conflict, and that this development was perfected by Beethoven. Now during the nineteenth century the danger to unity brought about by the intensification of contrasts, the rise of what we have called the technique of specific symbolization, and the continued tonal and harmonic expansion, required that new means of integration be found: among these, as we saw, were cyclical and related techniques, which ultimately culminated in Schoenbergian serialism.[1] But for composers who were interested in preserving the notion of conflict there sometimes arose the problem of how to secure strong contrasts in an idiom in which the principle of tonality as a means of obtaining and integrating these contrasts was losing its force, and in which *theme* was increasingly carrying the burden of unification. One solution, which was gradually discovered, was to separate the idea of conflict from the old formal and objective polarities on which it had formerly depended, and to make it rest on other factors, other techniques.

Precisely what these other factors are we can best indicate by invoking a concrete instance. In Sibelius's Second Symphony the new dualistic principle is fully in operation. Lacking the vocabulary to describe this phenomenon, commentators' verdicts about how this symphony's first movement "works" have differed widely. Cecil Gray, for instance, pointing to "the introduction of an entirely new principle into symphonic form", feels that this derives in part from the fact that "the convention of first and second subjects or groups is abandoned; in this movement one can detect several distinct groups of thematic germs none of which can claim the right to be regarded as the most important."[2] Gerald Abraham believes that the essentials of the movement are "the preservation of the superficial appearance of orthodox sonata-form and the substitution for the old sonata principle ... of [a] new principle of synthesis".[3] But the desperate search for a "proper" second subject has led one commentator to cite an insignificant thematic suffix played on the woodwind at cue B:

There are different opinions about which motif constitutes the second theme, and also, though to a lesser extent, about the main theme. The first motif in the woodwind ... would undoubtedly appear to be the main theme and the [above mentioned] motif the second theme ... This conviction is based in the first place on the fact that this motif is best suited to serve as the second theme as it offers a greater contrast to the main theme than any other thematic idea. Further, it and it alone is unmistakably in the key of the dominant ..., which in theory as well as in practice is so characteristic of a second theme. The motif at letter C on page 8, accepted by some as the second theme, is much too aggressive in character and lacks that quality of comparative calm which usually distinguishes the second theme of a sonata ...[4]

Abraham is close to the truth in observing that while the movement follows, at least superficially, an orthodox pattern, there is none of the usual dualistic interest. But the principle of synthesis that he mentions (close to the method of Borodin's First Symphony in which "all [the] thematic fragments are really parts of a single idea" stated for the first time in the coda) is less the real substitute than is the new principle of conflict.

The starting point for these various commentators is that there is no easily perceived, objective antithesis. What is most plausibly the formal "second-subject" stage—the *poco allegro* in F sharp minor at cue C—contains the same pulsating, repeated-note accompanimental figure that had characterized so much of the "first subject's" accompaniment and had opened the symphony. Indeed, this "second subject" seems to belong to the "first subject", to be another member of its group; it is just one of the melodic ideas that have been proliferating since the start. An attentive listener is likely to feel that it is part of the "first group" and that the "second group" is still to arrive. Unless he is unusually attentive: for then he will be already caught up in the work's drama on another plane: the conflict between the broad evolution of the music and what we might call its own *internalized principle of self-opposition*. The first suggestion of such a conflict is felt at the sudden hiatus eight bars after A. The flow of the music is broken unexpectedly; after an interval of seven crotchets the flutes try to set the music in motion again, but their short-windedness and their surprising twist to the minor succeed only in conveying an unmistakable forlornness:

EX. 4

A rest of four more crotchets intervenes before the bassoons introduce an asymmetrical upward-swinging phrase—not yet free of the tendency to the minor—as well as a change to C, which culminates in the menacing

EX. 5

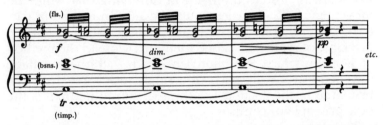

Now all this is rather astonishing and disturbing to the listener who from the very beginning had been caught up in the music's momentum, its melodic growth, and the increasing orchestral fullness and sonority. Minor though this first crisis is, it is not until the appearance of the "official" second subject some forty-one bars later (at C) that momentum, fullness, and confident thematicism are restored. The reappearance of the ostinato accompaniment, moreover, *for the first time since the crisis*, reinforces this feeling of restoration: clearly, this is no common "second-subject" opposition. The restoration is perhaps partial: the initial D major has after all been lost, and it will be some time before it is found again. The "second subject" has been in progress for no more than a few bars before one feels a growing sense of struggle—against distortion, fragmentation, tonal imbalance, and asymmetry.

But we need not go into this movement in any more detail, now that we have understood the principle that impels it. Broadly speaking, the development sees the process of disintegration and dismemberment taken to its furtherest degree, and the reassertion of the "second subject" leads to the relative tonal and thematic equilibrium of the recapitulation. But the struggle against distortion is carried through to the very closing bars: in all respects the principle of conflict operates quite

148

independently of the old dualistic formal precepts which are used in the movement.

What we have here, then, is a conflict between the music's declared "positives" and the factors that attempt to undermine them—not by objectively manifesting themselves but by revealing themselves only in terms of distortions effected upon those positives, as "symptoms" as it were. But before we attempt to comment on this new method, let us look at another example.

The final movement of Sibelius's Third Symphony is, as was pointed out earlier, a fusion of scherzo and finale. That tells us broadly what kind of movement it is and what general traditions lie behind it. But analysis of its details, and more particularly of its processes, becomes prob-lematic. It would be possible to describe the first part of the movement as follows:

> First group, in C major, up to cue 2; second group, in A minor, thereafter. At cue 3 a short transition, leading to a varied counter-exposition, with the second group now in F minor. Then development consisting mainly of first-group elements, but also of some elements from the second group. No recapitulation: instead, the next sec-tion, or last movement proper, preceded by murmur-ings of the new tune before it arrives.

The difficulty with this type of academic analysis is that it takes no cognizance of the fact that the section does not make that kind of impression on the listener; or, to put it another way, the organization and the principles involved are not *only* of that kind. For one thing, the section develops organically with motives appearing to derive from each other; in that sense we may speak of monism rather than dualism. The first part—the "first group"—strikes the listener as embryonic and exploratory, while the movement seems to begin properly only at the "second-group" stage: the former breeds the latter, and one feels no sense of objective dualistic antithesis between the "groups". Example 6 shows some of the principal thematic fragments of this exposition, and suggests the manner in which motives breed others:

EX. 6

The purpose of the example is to indicate how simple, unqualified talk of first and second subjects is here misleading: (f) is theoretically the first melodic fragment of the "second group", but it will be seen that it springs directly from the previous motives, and is no more different from any of them than most of them are from each other. The evolution is consistent from the start of the exposition, and the principle objectively monistic rather than dualistic.

For the business of this section is not to exploit any "contrast" between a "first" and a "second subject", but rather to come to terms with the processes of disintegration that are latent within it. In terms of this viewpoint, then, the collapse into fragments at cue 3 (the "transition") is the first positive manifestation of this internal conflict. The "symptoms" are the sudden athematicism, virtual atonality, fragmentation of previous elements, and chromaticism. Soon, however, the C pedal that was lost is found and a recovery follows. The next crisis is at cue 8, and the ensuing fragmentation functions as a development—though it should now be clear that it is both more and less than a development. The discovery of an E pedal at cue 12 and a half-hidden experiment with the big tune of the last section of the movement, or the "finale", leads to a restoration of C and a majestic statement of the new theme. This is the point of victory and its symbol: an apotheosis on a smaller scale than, but not qualitatively different from, the onset of the last movement of Beethoven's Fifth Symphony. We should note that adequate recognition of the effort and achievement of this *con energia* finale depends on our apprehension of the preceding struggle; the section has full meaning only in the context of our awareness of the music's attempt to find a melody of some stability, and the dissolution that follows as the concomitant of instability.

We are now in a position to state very generally the difference between the traditional technique of obtaining sonata dualism and this new technique. The old—the Classical—method entrusted dualism chiefly to objectively contradictory thematic and tonal wholes, which we customarily describe as "first" and "second subject": one theme manifestly contradicted another while being of course immanently, or latently, united to it. We may call this type *manifest* dualism. But in our new method, a motive may manifestly extend another—be related to it on the surface, as part of the music's spontaneous "flow"—while being immanently, beneath the surface as it were, a contradiction of it. We may call this new type *immanent* dualism. It was implicit in the sonata idea from the beginning; and there are even a few isolated examples of its explicit (if limited) use during the nineteenth century. We shall for the moment cite only two of these—both among the earliest instances. The first is Beethoven's *Eroica* Symphony. There the conflict in the first movement does not rest simply on incontrovertible tonal or thematic contradiction—hence, perhaps, the perennial fuss about "where the second subject begins". There is a second subject, certainly, but the point is that the second-subject function (antithesis) is not confined to what is officially called the second subject. The work uses "extra" thematic material (e.g. the new theme in the development) and thus has more diverse means of contrast than usual; but more important for our purposes is that some of the opposition to the first subject is *internalized within the subject itself*, as is borne out by the most important "symptom", the fall to C sharp in the seventh bar and all its subsequent implications. "The germ of the conflict", said Paul Bekker, speaking of the *Eroica*, "lies in the Hero himself".

In the first movement of Beethoven's Seventh Symphony the conflict is felt *before* the arrival of the second subject, as a latent (i.e. immanent) force that suddenly breaks the unshaken diatonicism of the first subject, troubling it, causing it to modulate away, pushing it to E major—the "proper" second-subject key—and beyond, to the flat submediant of that key. E major is thus both "symptom" and authentic opposition key. The drama is tonal rather than thematic: the second subject is closely derived from the first, a fact fully consistent with the operation of an immanent dualistic method. The movement is on the whole more monolithically tonal and diatonic than other first movements of its time; the drama derives from the attempts to undermine these huge (mainly tonic) key areas and so disturb their dance and song. The development is a struggle to regain the lost A major, which is exultantly regained, after a long period of mounting tension, at the recapitulation.

But to return to the twentieth century: both our examples have shown a dichotomy between form and function. Old sonata organization and new dualistic process have existed side by side—but remained more or less independent. One need hardly remark on the anomaly: traditional "dualistic" structure in a movement where duality does not rest upon that structure. This anomaly does not exist in all symphonies having recourse to the technique of immanent dualism, but it is nevertheless fairly common, and is to be found also in such familiar works as Vaughan Williams's Fifth Symphony, Sibelius's Fourth, and Prokofiev's Sixth. But where form and function are not identical, they can at least be made happily compatible: what normally happens, and what indeed happened in our first two examples, is that the second subject is overtly associated with the first and felt as a moment of temporary stability, or recovery, in the continuing struggle against the immanent forces of disintegration.

Consider the first movement of Prokofiev's Sixth Symphony in this light. The two principal themes of the movement—the main representatives of the first and second groups respectively—do not conflict in any sense; rather, they complement each other:

EX. 7

The first cry of anguish is the result of the workings of an immanent dualism that distorts the first subject into the passage beginning

EX. 8

Now it is precisely the recovery that precipitates the (modal) second-group stage, a moderato section that is felt to stand in sharp contrast to the preceding turmoil—being itself such a constrainedly lyrical lament—but whose overt sympathy with the previous group is perceived immediately. The next encounter with the latent principle of negation is direct and sudden, and the sharpest yet; it occurs at cue 13 and starts what is descriptively the central development of the movement.

But the demands of the old form and the procedures of the new technique can be brought into closer union than this. Indeed, sometimes the contrasting techniques of manifest and immanent dualism are made to complement each other, not by reducing the potency of either, but by making the second subject appear as a consequence of the operation of the latent negative on the first subject. In other words, the first subject is undermined and perverted from within, and then in its perverted form it turns upon itself and functions as second subject.

It is this special ambivalence that accounts for the problematic nature of the second group in the first movement of Mahler's Ninth Symphony. Some analysts (for instance Erwin Stein),[5] feel that the *etwas frischer* section in the exposition is the second-subject stage. This section, first encountered seven bars before cue 3 and differing not in key but only in mode (D *minor*) from the first subject (D *major*), is characterized by its new and relatively high dynamic level, its restless thematic line, and its triplet fanfare. For others (for instance Redlich)[6] everything in the movement is generated organically from the opening bars, and consequently no meaningful second group exists.

These two accounts seem to be in direct opposition—but there is truth in both of them. The "second group" certainly emerges as a mere melodic proliferation of what has gone before, and on its first appearance offers no tonal opposition by being in the tonic minor; but at the same time this "group" *does* assume an individual life, and a structural importance, during the movement, and is consistently used in opposition to the first group. Thus dualism depends both on one's perception of objectively contrasting thematic groups, and one's own subjective identification with what happens to a single theme or group, and how it is affected by some apparently latent opposite within itself. That is, dualism here partakes of both methods.

The movement *is* objectively monistic, and we have a "subjective" apprehension of an internal or immanent contradiction when the "first group's" blissful major diatonicism is disturbed ten bars after cue 2, causing *that same group* to turn minor, become restless and louder, and to yield further proliferations. But the movement *is* also "objectively" dualistic, for those proliferations acquire, during the course of the movement, a separate, independent life, and come to be used as a "second group" in opposition to a "first group".

But this objectification into "groups" takes place *later*: initially we hear only one thematic complex. The "second group's" evolutionary relationship to the "first" is made very clear in the recapitulation, where it emerges directly and naturally out of the first, sounding like a continuation of it that has suddenly turned to the minor.

This is by no means an isolated instance of collusion between our two dualistic techniques. Others are not hard to find: we shall mention two of them, in the hope that further discussion might clarify the principles and processes involved. Very much in the manner of Mahler's Ninth, the first movement of the Sixth Symphony by Karl Amadeus Hartmann is fundamentally a piece of musical monism which achieves duality through the use of two methods: an immanent agency distorts the once stable or "whole" thematic outline, and its harmonic and rhythmic corollaries, into various perversions; these perversions then achieve an ephemeral life of their own and are used in close alternation, or simultaneous contrapuntal deployment, with the original melody or with variations or even other perversions of it, in a manner approximating to the traditional opposition of autonomous themes.

The central theme of the movement, as given out by the cor anglais beginning in the sixth bar of the symphony (A^1 in the following example) is interrupted by the low rumblings on clarinet and piano and a rising chromatic run on the lower strings in the tenth bar, culminating in a high, disembodied motive in the first violins in the eleventh bar; this is an anticipation of the subject's first full-blown perversion, beginning in bar 17 (B^1 in the example). While at a simple descriptive level B^1 is of course a melodic extension and development of A^1, at the level that concerns us the relationship between B^1 and A^1 is subtle and complex, and difficult to rationalize, depending as it does so much upon a combination of factors—for instance, rhythm, outline, individual motives, total length, and the way these factors may have been expanded, or varied according to another principle.

EX. 9

In A² and B²—the analytical comparison of the two melodic shapes—three types of variation are noted, indicated by brackets *x*, *y*, and *z*. Type *x* is a free inversion, type *y* a free inversion with elaboration, and type *z* a transposition. Important notes in A¹ which are retained by B¹—allowing of course for transposition—are indicated by semibreves; notice that B¹ uses these important corner notes (or outline notes) at points of stress—i.e. at the beginning of bars. Notice also that melodies A¹ and B¹ have exactly the same length in terms of bars—and this despite the fact that some of the perversion worked by B¹ upon A¹ depends upon the fact that B¹ varies A¹ at a rate that is not consistent; i.e. it sometimes expands, sometimes compresses, A¹. The contrast brought about by the variations in B¹ are made definitive by the new string textures and by the volatile harmonic context they create.

Where a second subject is a perversion of the first it is part of a process at work on—or within—the first. Often one can pinpoint quite accurately the moment of its conception within the first subject: that moment will coincide with the first workings of an immanent dualism within that subject. In Sibelius's Fifth Symphony (opening movement) the moment of conception is bar 11. Suddenly the music turns minor; and the "new" subject is the precise shape eventually assumed by the music after the nine restless bars that ensue upon this critical moment.

EX. 10

This example should help to make clear how this "new" subject (b) is the "first" (a) in perverted form. Bracket *x* shows how the "first subject's" initial perfect fourth is preserved but that the interval between the outer notes is reduced from a perfect to a diminished fifth. And the whole figure is turned upside down. The "first subject's" next perfect fourth (bracket *y*) is also kept by the "second subject", but the latter's C-sharp now colours it with another diminished fifth—the sound of the tritone. Likewise, the first and last notes of (a) form a perfect fifth, while in (b) they are diminished. Ex. 10(c) shows another way in which the principal motive sounds through the "second" idea.

157

But there is a way by which the "problem" of the formal second subject—how to accommodate it with justification—can be made to fall away altogether. And that way is obvious enough: it is to let the second subject itself fall away. Sibelius, who made greater use of the technique of immanent dualism than any other composer, provides examples here too. We have already dealt with his Sixth and Seventh Symphonies from the formal point of view, noting among other things the absence of "subjects" from the first part of these works. We are now in a position to understand that it is precisely the functioning of a new dualistic technique that enables us to answer in the affirmative a question such as: is it possible that dualism (or conflict) can be obtained in an idiom which posits no conflict between themes, groups, or tonalities?

II

In symphonies that use the immanent dualistic principle we shall sometimes find, in addition to symptoms of its operation, a specific musical entity—say an interval—that is objectively in conflict with the given positives of the music, though it may very well be embodied by those positives. To the extent that this entity behaves as an objective antithesis it will remind us of the orthodox second subject; but in the light of what we know about the immanent principle we will be led to think of it as the internalized factor *in a state of partial externalization*.

A clear example is Walton's First Symphony. The opening is peaceful, but the agitated violin rhythms suggest a latent nervous tension. In the twelfth bar a hint dropped almost inaudibly by the cellos and basses is immediately embodied in the horn harmony: it is a flat seventh (A flat touched in the context of B flat), and it is of central importance to the business of this symphony:

EX. 11

Before this moment it is uncertain whether the tonality is to be major or minor, but now, as if by some dim presentiment, the key suddenly becomes B flat minor. The seventh, expressed in interval terms as a minor seventh, is taken into and made a function of the orchestra's steadily broadening crescendo, and contributes to the mood of rising excitement. Towards the apex of the crescendo, the horns and lower strings begin a series of quickening leaps away from the B flat tonic, reaching ever higher, until, at the moment of greatest confidence, the flat seventh is touched. Suddenly the music is thrust off its hitherto unshakeable pedal B flat, and onto a G pedal. With defiant persistence the flat seventh is maintained, the cello-bass figure from the opening (Ex. 11) is given out *fff* and when after twelve further bars the pedal jumps to C, the mood and orchestral texture are immediately fractured. This disruption of the increasingly confident and majestic stride of the music is felt keenly, and it is the nature of this disruption that provides the starkest symphonic contrast. For the struggle of this symphony is an attempt to come to terms with the contrary elements that are bent on undermining it. The dualism lies in the opposition of the "positive" force of wholeness and growth to the "negative" force of disintegration. This "negative" force is immanent of course, lying within the domain of the principal subject itself; yet it can be characterized by reference to the flat seventh *as its partial externalization*. And a keen paradox of this symphony lies in the fact that the flat seventh, while an aspect of the music's principle of undoing, is also indispensible to the music's own self-assertiveness.

The negative B flat–A flat syndrome forms an important part of the second subject's concern:

EX. 12

The third subject, a melody of tremendous striving,

emerges out of the presiding disorder, though remaining somehow still part of it, and embodies the interval of the seventh again—in both its major and minor forms, however. Since it has sharpened the minor seventh to major, and also goes through the major seventh into the octave, this subject seems to represent a spirit of correction; it participates in the struggle of the music to regain composure (and temporarily manages even to change the E pedal to F, the dominant of the home key):

EX. 13

This theme is effortful and energetic in search of the principal motive. This motive is finally restated—in A flat (or G sharp, as it is first notated). But this is the flat seventh of the home key once again, and treacherous ground: clearly the peace and order cannot remain for long.

In like manner the immanent—though partly externalized—drama is pursued throughout the four movements. The inherent agents of destruction gain full control in the *con malizia* second movement. This generic scherzo is in a kind of Dorian E, with the flat seventh prominent both vertically and horizontally—and stressed as such in the very first bar:

EX. 14

The finale brings the conventional resolution. The fugal second subject expresses the B flat–A flat syndrome again (*x* in Ex. 15)—though this is now happily reconciled in the new key of E flat, where it is no longer a local flat seventh. But this new key also has a tendency to touch on its own flat seventh, though it is now able to "correct" itself at once (*y*):

EX. 15

A flat seventh finally "corrected" diatonically: the component and the procedure are identical to that in Vaughan Williams's Fifth Symphony. Here again we have a dualistic process that is both immanent (because hidden, or "internal"), and partly manifest (because an objective antithesis is exposed within the subject-matter itself, as though this were a partial externalization of the hidden factor). The first movement opens serenely but the presence of a persistent and unresolved modal flat seventh gives an ambiguity, and the vaguest hint of instability, to the apparent D major:

EX. 16

But is is only later, at the end of the exposition and especially during the development, that the truly disruptive implications of this trait, this hint, become apparent. Here the interval of the second, implicit in the opening with its tonic and unresolved flat seventh, is realized horizontally in both its major and minor forms; it generates contrapuntal dissonances, and the prevailing instability is emphasized also by the frequently changing tonal centres. The C–D syndrome recurs in the scherzo: in some passages even at the original pitch, but also in a transposed horizontal representation in its minor form in each of the two episodes:

EX. 17

161

The finale takes the drama into its final stages. The famous "alleluias" were implicit in, and are a glorification of, those sections of the first movement where the "problematic" interval of the second was realized horizontally:

EX. 18

Eventually the music becomes obsessed with two alternating notes: these turn out to be the original D and C, and as the music slips over into the beginning of the first movement again, we realize that the process of melodic evolution has led us back to the point where we started. But the original dualism is not finally inescapable. In the coda, at last, the flat seventh is resolved, and the strings pile up in a sustained polyphony, reaching ever higher, embodying the "alleluias".

Of all "partly externalized" factors that one could imagine in the immanent dualistic method, perhaps none is so striking or effective as the tritone—the interval most destructive of tonality (and diatonicism). The most famous instance of its operation in a symphony is Sibelius's Fourth. The tritone is present from the opening bars:

EX. 19

and it defines the contour of the line that we may, thinking genealogically, call the "second subject", though it is scarcely more than a continuation of the first:

EX. 20

There is no escape from the interval, but its power may at least be temporarily suppressed as the melody resolves its force horizontally:

EX. 21

When not thus controlled, it tends to unleash such terror as reigns in the development, destroying not only tonality but any notion of wholeness. Such destruction happens again in the scherzo, where the tritone comes to be expressed *inter alia* in the polarization of the simultaneous tonal centres of F and B—a lethal rivalry that leaves the movement in fragments. The finale manages to soften dynamically, and reduce to the interval of a third, the piercing woodwind tritone calls of the development of the first movement:

EX. 22

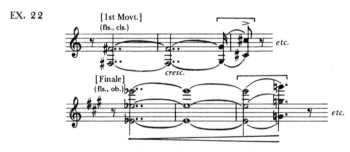

But that is not the full picture. For finally the symphony does not resolve the tritone. The work's triumph is that it succeeds in winning through to a creative involvement with the tritone, realizing for instance the architectonic potential of the interval, as it does when it brings together A major and E flat major twice over a considerable length in the final movement.

III

Discussion of "partial externalization", as we have called it, leads us to an important speculation. It is this. If in the technique of immanent dualism a musical cell can, in certain circumstances, behave in such a way that it seems to be a manifestation of part of the inherent and hidden antagonistic principle, then there ought to be occasions when we can speak of the *total* manifestation of a (formerly) hidden antagonism. If this were to happen, we would say that within the bounds of a single work, or even a single movement, immanent dualism had given way to manifest dualism: that the new symphonic technique had yielded the old.

This is not an idle speculation. There are a number of works in which it seems that precisely this shift—this process of "uncovering"—takes place. One of these is Nielsen's Sixth Symphony. In its first movement, the second subject is the outcome of an exploration of the first group: it is a "discovery" about the group, and explicitly about one particular subject in the group. In this sense it is a full externalization of a hostile trait inherent in the subject and thus its principle of undoing.

Ex. 23 is the first subject of the first group:

EX. 23

It carries with it a delicate clarinet and bassoon cascade, and before it is done it has introduced a minor tension into what was a crystalline G major. This is no serious symptom; but when the second idea of the group—

EX. 24

—carries the music away from G major and initially into C major, presentiments of unease are not slow in being expressed by the orchestra: the full significance of this apparently innocuous trait only steadily becomes clear as it is realized that the lost G major is unrecoverable. It also becomes clear that it is precisely the lost G major that is being sought, but that the closest the music is able to get is to keys semitonally adjacent to G. By the time the third idea of the group has been generated the prevailing centre is E flat:

EX. 25

Evidently the latent characteristic of the group, most clearly symptomized by its second member, is taking us further from the pure, diatonic G major of the opening. Ex. 26, however, offers itself in objective opposition to the preceding ideas:

EX. 26

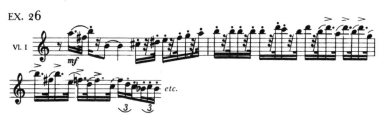

But related as this new subject is to the group—and particularly its second member—by its use of a similar staccato ostinato rhythm, a repeating-note tendency, a general scalic movement, and a shift away from the original tonality towards the sentence-end, it is easily felt as an *objectification* of a formerly immanent trait of the group. It is worth remarking that this "discovered" or "revealed" theme virtually supersedes its principal progenitor: apart from a couple of passing and distorting references during the ensuing development, Ex. 24 does not reappear. Or one may say that, purged from the first group, it reappears only as the undisguised second subject, i.e. as Ex. 26. During the subsequent development Ex. 26 insists on its connection with Ex. 24 by incorporating its most characteristic features and making itself the basis of a passage in the style of Ex. 24. The development is replete with brilliant juxtapositions and fusions; one of its admissions is that the formerly inherent tendency, though not symptomized in the pristine Ex. 23 as it was in Ex. 24, belonged to it nevertheless:

EX. 27

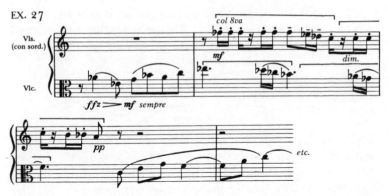

In such a work, then, immanent dualism turns into manifest dualism. Better still, the closest possible logical connection develops between the two; they seem but necessary stages in the working out of the symphony's central concern. Thus in addition to the two ways mentioned earlier, we have now a third way of uniting the new symphonic technique to the old. A consequence of the greatest importance follows from this last method of unification. It is that the existence of the (formal) second subject is hereby *justified*. If duality is implicity proposed by a first subject, and if the concealed antithesis is afterwards brought to the surface and laid bare in the form of another subject, one has orthodox sonata polarity in which both themes appear *rational* rather than formalistic. This is not to deny that the other ways (discussed earlier) of linking the new technique to the old format may also carry the possibility of justifying the old form; but nowhere is that potential as explicitly realized as here, where a second subject appears as the "objectification" of an impulse experienced "subjectively" within the first. We have then to revise slightly the general reasons, offered earlier, for the existence of the immanent dualistic technique. This technique, we suggested, existed to reactivate dualism. We see now that it may also exist to reactivate *form*.

Shostakovich's Tenth Symphony is one of that composer's Classically oriented works. The first movement is especially interesting as an instance of sonata form being made—through the means we have been considering—a viable medium in the mid-twentieth century. The *raison d'être* of its second subject is that it is the early externalization of an initially latent impulse. A superficial descriptive analysis of the exposition might run as follows. The first group begins immediately and continues until the entrance of the second group at cue 17, by which time it has undergone some development—of the kind typical of the composer, but including some of a more Classical kind as well. The tonal starting point of the first group is E minor; and the second group, a waltz clearly gleaned from one of the accompanying figures in the preceding development, is centred in Classically orthodox fashion around the relative G. Now those changes do make this a distinctive contrast to the bulk of the first group; but (and this points to the inadequacy of our merely empirical analysis) to an attentive listener it is not the critical contrast, not the one that impells the symphony forward: he will have discovered the truly generative contrast in the first few bars of the symphony.

One thing at least that we cannot fail to notice about the opening fifty-or-so bars of the movement is the periodic occurrence of the whole-measure caesuras, which interrupt the flow of the music; and if we are listening sensitively we will also notice that after each caesura the music strives to project itself in a new direction—both tonal and melodic—and into a new mood. Thus the first two bars, introducing the core of the first group, begin and end in the sphere of E minor. Then follows one bar of silence. The next burst of music (eleven bars) takes us into the region of the mediant G; it begins with a feeling of G minor, and ends by touching on the major. It also introduces important new material. The turn to the relative major is felt as a sudden brightening of the prevailing gloom; it is here that the next paragraph begins (i.e. in G major, and even brighter), and it manages to remain in this area for the next fifteen bars despite attempts to distract it; it also introduces a striking note of warmth and lyricism. After these fifteen bars the new mood is successfully destroyed by the original and prevailing gloom: G major vanishes, as do the warmth and lyricism, and we are back with a restless and preoccupied ennui. The next paragraph (i.e. after the intervening caesura) begins once again more optimistically in F sharp major: the mezzo-forte reached in the fifth bar is the highest dynamic yet. The next two caesuras are only of one crotchet (equivalent to one beat) each, and see a sudden acceleration of the pulse from ♩ = 96 to ♩ = 108, and a return to G minor; and then occurs the most unequivocal and striking contrast yet, as the elusive light, warmth and lyricism that had been suggested earlier are embodied in a rounded clarinet melody of affecting simplicity in the context of G major and aeolian E.

Up to this point the struggle between light and dark (the metaphors seem appropriate here) may quite correctly be described as being on the plane of immanent dualism. But now—even though the material is still clearly derived from the "first group" and indeed from the opening bars—we may wish to qualify this description in respect of the new theme, for it appears that the immanent tendency to "lighten" has externalized itself into an independent melody, a melody that is to fulfil a life and "bear a destiny" of its own in the ensuing drama. This new theme is of course the formal (but far from formalistic) second subject. The coda is a varied return of the opening bars, and as such places the conflict again on the "subjective" plane, where it first began; now, however, the progress from subjectivity to objectivity is no longer possible, and the movement ends in its original E minor.

Now just as the technique of immanent dualism was implicit in the sonata style from the beginning, so also are there a very few isolated early cases where some form of the process of "externalization" seems to be in operation. In Schumann's Fourth Symphony there is no true immanent dualism; but there is an objective, manifest duality which quite clearly gains force and particularly when *new* features of the original antithesis are disclosed—features that were apparently suppressed at first. In the exposition of the opening movement, the second-subject stage is marked merely by the fact that the prevailing D minor is displaced by F major: there is no thematic contrast. In the development the first subject yields a powerful, strutting theme—evidently a characteristic it had kept hidden in the exposition. Then after a fermata a new, lyrical F major theme banishes the first subject: the fact that the key is F major seems to suggest that this is the true, or revealed, second subject, which had been suppressed in the monothematic exposition. Very soon first-subject figures interrupt it, and the real struggle of the development—between the fully externalized poles of the dualism—begins to take place. The recapitulation, insofar as it exists at all, confirms the lyrical theme of the development as the true second subject by substituting it, and the "correct" D major, for the exposition's mere shift to the relative major.

Mendelssohn's *Italian* Symphony provides another early instance of the use of "externalization"—though now its operation is closer to our twentieth-century example, because it functions, as expected, in association with an "internalized" dualism. In the first movement, the real, objective, dramatic dualism is precipitated by the introduction of the new theme at the beginning of the development. This theme grows directly and naturally out of the inter-subject transition, a restless, staccato, thematically embryonic passage which in the exposition had subverted E major to minor, forte to piano, and had destroyed the first subject's sunny mood. At the start of the development that passage is recalled and gives rise to this new, dry-boned, minor-key fugato theme; hence it may be said to exist in a state of internalization in the exposition, and to gain externalization here. It is tonally restless, and at war with the first subject. It returns with its subverting power in the coda, but is ultimately suppressed by the first subject—though it is ominously present *within* the first subject, motivically, a few bars before the end. This opposing element proves finally inescapable: there are "subliminal" disturbances in the third movement; and the finale, clearly relating to that ominous "third subject" of the first movement as its full implication, comes to an end in exhaustion and despair.

The process of externalization of an internalized principle is at its most suggestive when it occurs at a *late* stage in a symphony or a symphonic movement, as part of the symphony's effort to resolve the dualism that preoccupies it. Here the act of externalization is potentially a very significant moment in the symphonic undertaking: it may suggest symbolically the attainment of a newfound clarity and objectivity, inasmuch as the "problem" that the symphony was wrestling with subjectively—immanently— has now been "understood" sufficiently for it to be stated objectively—externally—as a manifest dualism.

This new objectivity is certainly the implication of the two-subject sonata scheme that appears at a late stage—for the first time—in the single-movement Seventh Symphony by Sibelius. The original conflict is internal, and is adumbrated in the first few bars of the symphony:

EX. 28

There is the optimistic upward-sweeping figure; it is diatonic, has a unisonal strength, involves a crescendo, and appears unchallenged. But without warning it is cut off: the chromatic intrusion in the third bar—at the distance of a tritone from the preceding unison—is a sudden and annihilating catastrophe; woodwind, horns and strings play out the aftermath chromatically. Soon equilibrium (expressed again as diatonic stability) regains control and a new assertion of optimism follows—a reversal that establishes the internal struggle of the symphony.

In summary the course of the work is as follows. The opening adagio presents the dualism immanently, but an ensuing *vivacissimo* fully succumbs to its perverting power. A brief second adagio restores the balance by asserting one of the music's "positives" (a trombone theme) over turbulent, chromatic string lines which are redolent of the hidden "negative". But the allegro "finale" manages to pose the antithesis objectively, to externalize it in terms of contrasting subjects: the conflict is brought to the surface— "out of the unconscious", one is tempted to say. The process of examination and struggle—i.e. of development, in a real sense of this word—has externalized the negative force in the shape of Ex. 29:

EX. 29

It is clearly related to an idea in the *vivacissimo*:

EX. 30

—though the new shape has far greater definition. To an important degree this symphony's concern has been to objectify the subjective factor in its dualism; the objectification, it seems, is an important stage in its deeper concern to come to terms with it. The finale can thus approach the conflict with something like Classical objectify the subjective factor in its dualism; the objectification, it seems, is an important stage in its deeper also mention Sibelius's Sixth Symphony—another example of an immanent conflict becoming manifest in the finale: the externalized thematic and tonal opposites are allowed full expansion in terms of a highly intricate but basically tripartite structure, with coda. The second of these retains the character of subversiveness, and occupies the central section, beginning at cue B: it offers a dramatic and unequivocal contrast after the almost liturgical peace of the first section.

As one might expect, this procedure—the late externalization of a formerly internal factor—is apparently an exclusively twentieth-century phenomenon. But one notable exception has come to light: an early nineteenth-century work, in which a very similar type of process takes place. The work is Beethoven's Seventh Symphony. Its slow introduction is a symbolic welter of confused tendencies, impulses, directions. There are many implications here which are neither explored nor, at this stage, "understood". There is a great deal of latent conflict. And it is this conflict which the Symphony "composes out" over its four movements, exploring different aspects of it in turn (and thereby in turn suppressing others) until all can be presented and harmonized openly. We saw earlier in this chapter that the first movement presents the opposites mainly in terms of key. The second (allegretto) movement then presents them mainly in terms of theme: the alternating sections contrast thematically but have a key centre (A) in common, and in common with the previous movement also. The scherzo has both tonal *and* thematic contrast—but without interaction. But in the finale both characteristics are fully present, fully externalized, and interacting, for the first time. In this sonata movement neither thematic or tonal elements exist in a state of suppression.

NOTES

[1] cf. Friedheim, Philip; "The relationship between tonality and musical structure", *Music Review*, February 1966, Vol. 27 No. 1 pp. 44–54. Also, Keller, Hans; "Sonata and symphony today", *Music Review*, May 1961, Vol. 22 No. 2, p. 172.

[2] *Sibelius; the symphonies* ("The Musical Pilgrim Series"), London 1931, pp. 134–135.

[3] *Sibelius: a Symposium*, p. 19.

[4] Parmet; *The Symphonies of Sibelius*, p. 19.

[5] *Orpheus in New Guises*, p. 20.

[6] *Bruckner and Mahler*, p. 227.

5
Symphonic conflict further redefined

I

By convention, counterpoint is monistic. Traditionally it comes to life within a fabric whose unity and cohesion are taken for granted. Contrapuntal lines, we might say, complement each other. But what if such a line should rebel? What if a counterpoint should so far protest its individuality that it comes into *conflict* with its context? And what if this line should then associate itself with a characteristic instrumental colour, in opposition to other lines characterized by different instrumental colours? Clearly, these possibilities suggest two new means by which dualism might be generated. Beyond the traditional dualistic method of disjunct, contrasting keys and themes, beyond the technique of immanent dualism which we discussed in the previous chapter, we begin this chapter with an examination of some twentieth-century symphonies that have made viable symphonically a dualism founded on one or both of these two further principles: counterpoint and timbre.

It has already been argued (Chapter 3) that Roy Harris's Third Symphony is a "textural" piece without any compromise with "shape"; that it is a perpetual evolution in which everything springs from the opening unisonal chant. Where, within this monistic technique of linear evolution, is there room for duality? We shall not find the answer by searching for concealed "subjects". Rather, the conflict in the symphony lies between the contrapuntal lines it develops in the course of its growth. The procedure is unmistakable; its initial development is clear and convincing. The opening cello plainsong is without tension;

but the innocence of this primeval quasi-pentatonic
monody is to be gradually challenged and "corrupted" in a
musical development that imitates the historical evolution
of monody into organum, higher forms of polyphony,
secular song, fugue, and beyond, showing in dramatic
musical analogy the growth of Western civilisation and the
challenge to innocence through the tensions and conflicts
that growth inevitably brings. At first there is just the cello
line. Then the violas enter, sustaining the last note of each
cello phrase, and hence in *alternation* with the cellos. There is
a sensation of tearing at the seams when the parts, in search
of individuality, abandon unison and parallel octave
movement and touch notes a fourth or a fifth away from
the melody notes; they are immediately forced back into
unison and octave—only to struggle away once again:

EX. 31

The search of the parts for greater individuality continues,
moving into types of organum, more complex polyphony
and further, and bringing with it increased tension between
the parts and a growing sense of conflict. The lines expand,
proliferate, develop into several counterpoints, interact,
generate crises, undergo metamorphoses.

The tensions and conflicts between the strands in this
polyphonic web are frequently sharpened and emphasized
by a clear antagonism between instrumental groups: thus
timbre also enters into the service of symphonic dualism.
While tending to heighten the principal features of the
dramatic conflict, this does not obscure the subtler polyphonic aggravations such as might occur between the

parts of a homogeneous instrumental group itself. From about cue 10 the conflict tends to align itself along a clear woodwind-strings polarity. After the crisis at cue 13 relative calm prevails for a few bars until with gradually mounting tension the polyphonic conflict of woodwind–strings characterization resumes its struggle—though now in the presence of a third conflicting group, horns and trumpets; the struggle hence becomes tripartite. At the same time, an examination of the string group in this section will show that the tensions within that group itself—i.e. between the lines that provide its full texture—are not ignored because of the broader characterization.

This woodwind–strings polarity is maintained also in the ensuing "section" (from about cue 21), wherein metamorphosis and evolution have changed the basic idea so far that it is rendered with the rhythm and clipped periodicity of secular song. At length the same third party— horns and trumpets, soon joined by trombones—enters menacingly and quickly undermines the woodwind, whose melody it adopts immediately afterwards. With the first woodwind rally, led by the flutes, tensions quickly develop once more and a major crisis is precipitated. The fugue develops conflicts between strings and woodwind on the one hand, and brass and percussion on the other. Again, there are strong tensions *within* each group, expressed in the characteristic canonic working. The "coda" goes some way towards reconciling the contrapuntal-cum-instrumental conflicts and attempting to resolve them into a more homophonic entity—though now we are in the presence of a remorseless funereal thud in the timpani, and the tragic implications are unmistakable.

As we might expect, the use of tonality in this work is not dramatic in the ordinary symphonic sense. Tonality is used more in accordance with the demands of "textural" procedure than as a means of sectional opposition. Nevertheless key has a vital role; for if tonality is here the result of the proliferation of line, it is also a means of supporting the particular method of creating conflict: it enhances the individuality of the lines and generates tension between them. This is noticeable in the bitonality in Ex. 32

where, at the climax of the first "section", the opposition between the lines is emphasized not only by their contrasting instrumental characterization (violins on the one hand, woodwind supported by lower strings on the other) but by their conflicting tonal tendencies:

EX. 32

Nor, of course, is there any Classical development here—instead there is simply evolution and permutation. Though the process is that of linear, polyphonic growth, there is still a sense in which the ideas "have to bear a destiny of their own"; and, in a way that is true of the Beethoven symphony, the cells develop and undergo significant permutations as a result of conflict.

The techniques of the Third Symphony are not unique; they are to some extent characteristic of Harris, and reappear for instance in the Seventh Symphony. But from one point of view both of these works are simple, in that they are *sui generis*. They are "textures"; in neither of them is there any compromise with traditional symphonic "shapes": thus there is no problem of reconciling the new dialectic of counterpoint and of timbre with the presuppositions of received forms. A work that very successfully achieves this reconciliation is Alexander Goehr's *Little Symphony*; in this sense it is more complex than either of the Harris symphonies. Its way, we might say, is to "rationalize" conventional forms; at first it is primarily involved with contrapuntal procedures, but increasingly it separates out the conflicting counterpoints and organizes them into "forms".

The conflictive issues of the symphony are complex and

various. They rest principally on oppositions between lines or textures—either in vertical or horizontal relationship or both—which are strongly emphasized by instrumental characterization so that there arise what appear as opposing instrumental protagonists. The first movement is a brief preludial chorale; in the second movement, a series of eighteen variations on the chorale, the method of using a distinctive instrumental "registration" for each variation assists in defining the contrasts *between* the variations when such are intended—though such sectional contrasts are less important as a means of conflict in this movement than contrapuntal contrasts. Likewise the use of members of contrasting instrumental families *within* many of the variations assists in defining the internal (mainly vertical) conflicts. Sometimes the internal polarity rests on the vertical opposition of one line against several—i.e. a single strand against a whole texture, in which case a solo instrument or an instrumental sub-group (say violas, or obocs) is pitted against a number of instruments of the same family or of contrasting orchestral families. Instances of this are Variation II, where violas oppose oboes and clarinet:

EX. 33

or Variation IV, where a solo tuba opposes a thick texture made up of clarinet, bass clarinet, horns and strings. Sometimes this internal polarity rests on the vertical opposition of groups of lines, or textures, usually characterized by broadly similar, though often mixed, groups of instruments—for instance Variation XII, where oboe and clarinet support each other, without merely doubling, in their argument with violins and cellos:

EX. 34

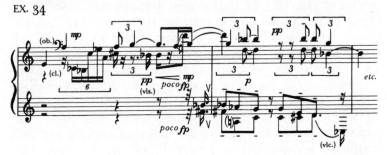

or Variation XIII, where the brass instruments (i.e. horn and tuba), reinforced by all the woodwind (i.e. piccolo, oboes, clarinet, bass clarinet) engage in a forceful battle with the strings. In cases where one of the antagonistic groups is distinctly smaller than the other and is soloistic in nature, the resemblance to a *concertino-ripieno* scheme is perfectly clear. Vertical opposition is at its simplest in Variation IX (the central variation, if one includes the original chorale in one's counting), where, apart from a three-note contribution in the middle from the clarinet, the entire variation is carried by the two horns.

Conflicting types of movement, or motion, are not separable from the kinds of conflict mentioned above, for they are among the factors that help to create those conflicts. However, tension between different types of movement is a factor of contrast, sectional or simultaneous (linear or textural), that is important enough in this symphony to demand mention on its own. Such conflicts are in this symphony greatly dependent on the motoric autonomy of the opposing entities which expresses itself for instance as a strong bi- or polyrhythmicality, or (and in the total view of the symphony the most important) as simultaneous or successive differing *rates* of movement (i.e. slow, fast, etc.). Something of this motoric autonomy may have been suggested by Exs. 33 and 34; still restricting ourselves for the moment to the second movement, the following examples may help to make it clearer. Ex. 35 shows the first part of Variation III where the rapid piccolo figurations contrast strikingly with the much slower moving violin line and where a great tension between the two results on this count alone.

EX. 35

A rhythmic skeleton of most of Variation XIII, which was mentioned earlier, speaks for itself:

EX. 36

The third movement is generically the scherzo: a rapid ternary piece with a slower and simpler trio-like central section. The movement continues the vertical (i.e. contra-puntal) articulation of conflict, but now also makes con-siderable use of sectional contrasts. Vertical opposition—with the attendant motoric autonomy—is once again supported by a clear and consistent instrumental characterization:

EX. 37

And in its sectional expression, conflict exists between sharply differentiated sections: between the hectic scherzo (in a traditional 3/4) and the lightly scored, limpid and lyrical trio, overtly derivative of the first movement chorale, and fluctuating between 2/4 and 3/4. The fourth movement organizes the conflict in a predominantly sectional way for the first time in the work: the issues have evidently been clarified to the point at which they can be thus separated—a process closely similar to the externalization of internal factors in an immanently dualistic work. The outcome of the symphony will now depend on the more orthodox—because sectional—inter-action and working out of these conflictual issues.

In the Harris and Goehr symphonies, we have seen that instrumental affiliations may become highly functional in the characterization and working out of a symphonic dialectic founded primarily on counterpoint. The question that now therefore urges itself upon us is this: is it possible that a symphonic argument could be sustained in which such instrumental affiliations were the principal terms of the conflict?

Iain Hamilton's Sinfonia for Two Orchestras offers a brilliant and affirmative answer. Symphonic conflict here depends on the delineation of opposing instrumental groups which are also inter-locking (overlapping) because the members of each group have more than one affiliation. In other words the full and fairly standard symphony orchestra is broken down several ways—so that each instrument belongs to more than one group and that these sectional groups stand in a complex relationship to each other in conflict patterns of varying degrees of intensity. The work's business is to define these relationships, clarify and organize them; and by discovering in the process the unity that underlies the conflicting diversity, to reconcile the groups without destroying the individuality of any.

The "two orchestras" of the title derive from the division of what is a fairly normal symphony orchestra into two instrumentally balanced but contrasting groups. Indeed, once it is understood that the work is scored for what in reality is a single symphony orchestra, the duality stressed by the title in its insistence upon *two* orchestras is seen to be all the more significant. The two orchestras are:

I	II
2 flutes (2nd doubles piccolo)	2 oboes (2nd doubles cor anglais)
2 B flat clarinets (2nd doubles bass clarinet)	2 bassoons
4 horns in F	3 trumpets in C
tuba	3 trombones
percussion (suspended cymbal, tam-tam, glockenspiel, xylophone, celeste, bells)	timpani
	piano
	violins II
	violas
	basses
harp	
violins I	

These two orchestras represent the two major opposing protagonists. The other strongly defined and contrasted groups, whose divisions cut right across the main ones, are the major instrumental families: the percussion, the strings, the brass, and the woodwind, used in that order. The harp, piano and timpani further divide their allegiances: the harp and piano associate themselves with the strings (they are, after all, "strung" instruments), and the timpani lend support to the woodwind. The work has already been formally discussed in some detail (Chapter 3). To summarise: the Sinfonia consists of eleven short sections each of which is scored either for one of the main orchestral groups or for one of the "family" groups (whose sections are called *Tessiture*)—with the exception of the outer sections which are scored for the *tutti* orchestral ensemble. The contrast between the sections (and therefore between the instrumental groups) is underlined by the constant switches in tempo and metre from the one to the other. Clearly, then, the form of the work articulates its basic symphonic concern: the exploration of these multiple instrumental conflicts.

The symphony opens with a statement of tremendous tension; in its calling of the listener's attention to the real issues at hand it is an apt modern counterpart of the traditional exposition. The method and idiom are obviously different but the principle is the same. (In its sostenuto tempo it perhaps also retains something of the traditional slow introduction). This opening section is scored for both orchestras—the prime opposites—and it is their simultaneous deployment that creates much of the tension; but tension is also created by the divided allegiance we have spoken about, for across the physical space that delineates the two orchestral blocks, the related instruments throw out ties, attempt to demonstrate their relatedness by means of pitch and rhythmic-figure similarities, by temporal coincidences, and by means of imitation. In order to understand all this from a mere study of the score it is essential to remember that the opposing orchestras are so arranged on the stage that their distinctiveness and separateness is clearly seen and can be acoustically apprehended; according to the composer's instructions, thus:

Orchestra I   Orchestra II

Perc.   Timp.

Tuba   Cor.   Tbe.   Tbni.
Fl.   Cl.   Ob.   Fag.
Harp   Piano

Bassi

Celli   Viole
Violini I   Violini II

The avoidance of linear movement in every part, moreover, and the successive fortissimo entries of the different instruments, tends to focus attention on the contrasts and conflicts inherent in the sound textures:

EX. 38

I. Le due orchestre

183

In the clearly differentiated sections that follow, the contrasts are chronological (i.e. inter-sectional) as well as— or perhaps more than—simultaneous (i.e. intra-sectional). The latter are of course less present in the *Tessiture*, where conflict is at its lowest and concern with sheer texture at its highest, than in the orchestral sections, where instruments are often prepared to protest their individuality, frequently in ways that generate contrapuntal tension—as for instance in this passage from Section 2:

EX. 39

These sections—Nos. 2 to 10 inclusive—have affinities with traditional symphonic development: not stylistic or methodical but only "functional" affinities, in that they examine, extend, fully reveal and clarify the issues inherent in the first section. Such elucidation "makes possible" the reunion of the opposing orchestras in the penultimate section, and thereafter the melodic celebration in the last. Certainly there is no total resolution as in a Beethoven symphony; but one has at least the feeling that the systematic "development" and clarification of the basic tensions has enabled the opposing protagonists to take their place alongside each other with the equanimity that is the result of a clearer understanding of the fundamental unity that underlies their differences.

185

II

The concepts of immanent dualism, of a dialectic of counterpoint, and of instrumental and timbre conflict, have brought us a long way from the traditional symphonic notion of a duality between disjunct keys and themes. An important issue is involved here. Once we can accept the possibility of the dialectic of symphonic thought coming to life in terms of new polarities and by means of new procedures, there is in principle no limit to the number of ways symphonic thought may realize itself, except of course the limitations of music to sustain and communicate such thought. To be more specific: there is no reason in principle why the dialectic should not make itself felt as, say, structure; why, that is, the music's own *form* of coming into being should not be subject to countervailing demands or principles, and why therefore the conflict should not realize itself as *tensions internal to the music's own structural process*. Of the twentieth-century works that offer themselves for serious consideration in this connection we might single out four for discussion: all notable works in their own right, each approaching its task in a different way. They are the First and Second Symphonies by Tippett, Webern's Symphony Op. 21, and the First Symphony by Roberto Gerhard.

In Tippett's First Symphony the dualistic interest at its highest, most abstruse level, is the contradiction between *Form* and *Texture*[1]—but its presentation at the level of immediate perception begins as a study of the contrast and capacity for intense individualization of the contrapuntal lines in a textural idiom; to this extent the work follows on logically from our earlier discussion. In the allegro first movement the contrapuntal style itself is made the basis of conflict. It is the tension between the monistically derived yet strongly individualized—and ultimately conflicting—contrapuntal lines, and their offshoots, that is exploited. Ex. 40 shows the opening of the symphony; immediately the two basic contrapuntal lines are individualized thematically and rhythmically, and there is even a kind of tonal independence in the way the lower line tries soon to

turn away from the initial, and the upper line's, A major:
the lines are felt to be in opposition:

EX. 40

Of course these are not "entities" in the way that usual
symphonic subjects are—they are not easily detached from
their context—but are incipient contrapuntal lines in a
monistic style, lines that are continually to expand and
unfold into new but closely related patterns in a manner
akin to that of the sixteenth-century English polyphonists to
whom Tippett owes so much. Thus the antitheses are not
defined simply by the upper and lower lines of Ex. 40: each
of these reveals many new contours between which conflict
occurs in varying degrees. There is nothing that can
honestly be called a second subject here; but (and here is the
first compromise with a "shape" technique) the tension
between the lines forces the music dramatically out of the
area of A major into tonalities where the original key is
seriously challenged and indeed—in Tovey's phrase—sinks
below the horizon. This of course would not be likely to
happen in a *purely*, or traditionally, textural piece, where all
departures from the home-key would be moves into nearly
related regions that never seriously called into question the

home ground, and would in any case be incidental points in the evolutionary growth of the lines.

This tonal challenge is offered most forcefully by the development section—another compromise with "shape" —which differentiates itself from the exposition by virtue not only of its dramatic use of tonality but by the way it treats the foregoing textural section as a storehouse of ideas which it deploys in a recognizably symphonically developmental manner. The evolution of new contours is not the business of this development, in quite the way it was of the foregoing exposition: rather its business is to examine old ones. The full-scale recapitulation in the home-key is the next "shape" compromise—and re-capitulation it certainly is, for it does not merely restate the original contrapuntal ideas and then allow the lines to yield new consequences. It is a return and a restatement of the opening section—with, moreover, orthodox key adjustments in favour of the home-key, A major. To say that it is not literal in no way invalidates its orthodoxy.

The course of this symphony is one of gradual emergence from a basically textural idiom, through compromise with techniques of "shape", to an idiom governed by "shape", and finally back to texture through a reversal of these processes in the last movement. The adagio, in the key of the supertonic minor, thus begins at one remove from the more purely and autonomously polyphonic idiom of the opening of the first movement: it is a passacaglia, originally a dance form, and one resting upon the repetition of a ground, which in this case is a regular eight-bar sentence, with antecedent and consequent. Here there are two clearly differentiated themes: the ground, and the subject that expands and proliferates above it. The use of tonality is again dramatic in the sense that the modulations push the home-key below the horizon and even traverse distant territory: we are taken through D minor, F minor, C sharp minor, A minor, E minor (these last two in passing). And the return to the home-key is also dramatic and *accompanied by a restatement of most of the opening section*. This is a great compromise with "shape"—and it appears all the more so when it is discovered that the earlier section is now regarded so sectionally—so much as an "entity"—that its sentences can be recapitulated in reverse order. This reprise, apart from the reversal in order of presentation of what was previously a naturally evolving and expanding polyphonic texture, is largely literal, the only important change being necessarily in the concluding bars. By the third movement "shape" has gained the upper hand: it is a presto movement in orthodox scherzo-and-trio form. The more textural section is relegated to the middle, to the trio—a highly contrasting polyphonic passage for strings, which by setting out in D Dorian maintains D as the tonal centre of the movement.

The synthesis and resolution of the finale is that while it begins as a "shape" movement, with contrasting subjects, albeit extended polyphonically (texturally), it resolves itself back into a textural movement in which the formally contrasting subjects co-exist contrapuntally without friction. The first group consists basically of a subject and its counter-subject which are immediately extended and developed for several pages before they climax and give way to the second group. The latter is a contrasting section, predominantly piano, dolce, and piacevole, of fluctuating tonal centre but setting out in C dorian and expanding in a fugato treatment. Clearly, what we have in this exposition is a textural idiom which has been made subservient to the considerations of "shape"; as in the previous movement it is the "shape" which dictates—which is fundamental— though the idiom is now more polyphonic. This holds good also for the ensuing development, another prescription of the sonata "shape". Here both groups meet and are deployed contrapuntally and motivically, and it is here that texture once again gains control: the two groups find at length that they combine very well and thereafter there is no separating them. The motivic development ceases, the lines become whole once more, each with its own inherent life. It is a falsification to speak about this as recapitulation: it is a textural process that begins in the midst of the development, outside of the central tonality, and proceeds from there until A is brought round again—and according to principles that have nothing to do with the "shape"-

dominated exposition. It would even be a falsification to speak of a simultaneous recapitulation, for the use of the word "recapitulation" presumes a principle which does not pertain to what happens after about cue 12 of the finale. It is the resumption of a principally textural means of control, rather than a recapitulation (which implies a formal control), that is important. And it is not surprising that the regaining of the tonic major is not a dramatic event: it is merely an an incidental one in an inevitable organic process, a kind of growth which can therefore continue for as long as there is energy. As it happens, it goes on growing: the cycle continues beyond the resumption of A major, turning immediately towards E major (the dominant) where it ends.

Thus a work which began by creating a dualistic tension within a monistic idiom, by generating a dramatic conflict between the contrapuntal lines (and thence a contradiction between texture and "shape"), and which perpetuated these dualisms in various ways through the four movements, ends by resolving contrapuntal tension into a harmonious polyphony (and thence resolving "shape" back into texture). One may express the matter thus: the symphony's overriding concern with the contradictions between Form and Texture comes into being—or rather is made dramatically apprehensible—through the primary struggle between contrapuntal lines; as these contrapuntal lines conflict they disrupt the homogeneity of the polyphonic texture and create a need for a "shape" organization, for a control by Form; as they are reconciled the need for external Form disappears. This brilliantly original symphony is itself structurally a dramatic enactment of an important problem for the twentieth-century symphony: the dichotomy between the old dualistic practice and the monistic character of much twentieth-century musical language.

Like his First Symphony, Tippett's Second uses Form as an element which participates in the symphonic drama, almost as another subject, with a dynamic life of its own. The First Symphony's "problem" was the contradiction between Form and Texture, studied dramatically as the conflict between simultaneous (i.e. contrapuntal) and later sectionally disposed lines; the Second is concerned with a dialectic of *Form* and *Content*, and its immediate dramatic presentation involves the tensions within and between strongly individualized sections. Over a recognizably traditional ground-plan Tippett builds a work that deploys the basic formal "ingredients" to an end that is as unique as in his First Symphony. The work is in C major, and though it makes articulate use of contrasted tonal areas, between movements and within movements, key does not strictly speaking function as a vital generating and regulating factor in Tippett generally, and in this symphony in particular. That notion of key is temporal and progressive; for Tippett time and key are usually contingent rather than necessary.

We have already (Chapter 3) discussed the form of the outer movements of this symphony, but it is necessary now to re-state briefly some of the particulars that were mentioned then. The first movement is based in orthodox fashion on the contrast of two thematic complexes: the first, basically in C, is steely and rhythmical, while the second, initially in E flat, has pliable *carillonando* counterpoints. The two are further distinguished by means of timbre: the first thematic complex has mainly string, brass and piano textures, while the second belongs mainly to the woodwind. Though described by the composer as a "dramatic sonata allegro", the movement shuns traditional form in favour of a structure of four closely related main sections; Tippett calls them "statement, first argument, re-statement, second argument and coda". Far from being ordinary developments, the "arguments" are reviews of their preceding "statements" in which the earlier material is somewhat varied, reorganized (so as to yield a more complex, less symmetrical micro-structure), and extrapolated: thus the movement really presents the same fundamental material four times over, each time at almost exactly the same length. Form is the very heart of this movement, as it is of the symphony as a whole, and as it was of the First Symphony. Writing of the Second Symphony, Tippett has admitted the extent to which his compositional thinking generally is dominated and enticed by form:

> I prefer to invent the work's form in as great a detail as I can before I invent any sounds whatever. But as the formal invention proceeds, textures, speeds, dynamics, become part of the formal process. So that one comes closer and closer to the sound itself until the moment when the dam breaks and the music of the opening bars spills out over the paper.[2]

In this first movement Form is severe discipline—the rigid, constricting order imposed onto the music to hold the contrasts together and give coherence. Moreover, form is the external control that holds in check the music's inner tendency for dynamic expansion and diversification. At a deep level a tension results from this: one becomes aware that the structure is "not adequate" to the content. Each section (or micro-section) grows dynamically outward, always further away from its source; at climactic points it is interrupted by the start of another section—which is in fact not a culmination but a review of the same material (or in the case of a micro-section, quite new material). The spirit is energetic, while the form—the *discipline* essentially, in this case—is static: that, at the deepest level, is the conflict, and it is the central preoccupation of the symphony. And despite the discipline, the formal straitjacketing, each section manages over the course of the movement to develop; each section is affected by the experience of its predecessors; and the music manages to change, as if under the pressure of its repeatedly curtailed impulses.

In the more placid, relatively static slow movement—a lucid ternary structure with introduction and coda—the sectional song-form is Form more appropriate to the content. Tensions here are less—and traditionally so for a symphony. One may say that the movement represents a temporary concession to Form. The high energy of the third movement is required to take up the struggle again and shift the "balance": a rapid, rhythmically complex scherzo, in additive rhythm and in a very free rondo form, the movement retains some of the earlier repetitive sectionality but now the arching dynamic overrides all (the metaphor is apt, for the music rises to a central climax and falls thereafter). The breadth of the climax and the full and sufficient exhalation immediately after it (cue 112 *et seq.*) are striking, because so new, after the experience of the first movement. We have called the movement a free rondo, in order to show its proper genealogy; Tippett likes to call it an "additive structure", a phrase that is appropriate to its method of always rotating old material in transformation in the presence of new material. The issue is that, unlike in the first movement, the implications of the material are permitted to drive the movement on, "additively"—but still in the presence of some sectional, repetitional "check". This points the direction the symphony has taken and anticipates the full resolution of the last movement.

The four sections of the last movement implicitly refer to the four sections of the first movement; the composer himself has pointed out the connection. Unlike the first movement, which was given coherence by rigid Form, this movement places together four sections in apparently total disconnectedness; in a sense that has meaning for this symphony the movement is written *without* Form. For here the contrasts *hold themselves together*: the Content is *its own* Form; and our awareness of the latent interconnections between the sections of this (so-called) "fantasia" is a measure of our deeper intuition of the relatedness of free, apparently disparate entities. With this insight we have abandoned rigorous management of the separate facts before us; we have learnt to "see" the deeper relations, and control of the old kind has been rendered redundant. The four parts of the movement contrast not only in the usual matters of theme, and so on, but also in their formal "lives". The forms of the first three sections become progressively freer in themselves, representing symbolically the whole work's attempt to liberate itself from Form—i.e. from form-as-regulative-pattern. The first section is "additive" and repetitive in a way that recalls the third movement, the second (cue 144) is a passacaglia, and the third (cue 169) one vast, freely unwinding melody—in a sense the symphony's culmination, symbolically suggestive of the "achievement". The fourth section (cue 181)—which is coda as well—is a resolution of the symphony into a kind of *Urthema*; and it recalls the very beginning of the work. It is a single quintessential urge, made five times over for emphasis. Form here is apt, for unlike the first movement, which the principle of repetition recalls, the "shape" is fully in the service of the spirit—emphatic, cadential and ecstatically fulfilled. The fact that this section recalls the main theme of the first movement—and that movement itself—insisting that the end is the same as the beginning, makes the point that this is not a progressive, temporal drama in the Beethoven manner; though like Bruckner's symphonies, which also differ in a somewhat similar way, it still relates to the Beethoven ethic of achievement.

The contradictions explored in the Tippett symphonies—between Form and Texture, and between Form and Content—are less intellectual and esoteric than the structural antitheses that lie at the heart of the Symphony Op. 21 by Webern. This concise two-movement work (a sonata form followed by a theme and variations) is at a technical level pure monism, built as it is on the implications of a single tone row; but it unmistakably engages with the traditional symphonic ethic of musical dualism insofar as it is profoundly and uniquely involved with a polarity of *Symmetry* and *Asymmetry*. Its abiding preoccupation is a struggle against asymmetry and imbalance, in favour of perfect symmetry and balance—which it seeks in the perfect mirror forms of canon by inversion, and retrograde motion. In every section—i.e. in the exposition, development, and recapitulation of the first movement, and in the theme and its separate variations, and in the coda, of the second movement—symmetry is sought in retrograde movement; in every section except the final coda some sort of canon is attempted. The absence of canon from the final coda is significant, for it is in the last variation that asymmetry is finally defeated and symmetry reigns in the perfect and long-sought-for bi-unity of canon by inversion and retrograde motion. Hence the coda, with canon not attempted in any way for the first time in the piece, represents a new relaxation, a new simplicity, relying as it does purely on the symmetry of retrograde movement.

The basic set itself is such that it expresses the symphony's concern for symmetry—and the elusiveness of that symmetry. The row divides perfectly into two halves, and the second half is a perfect retrograde of the first. Yet plainly the *symmetry* is far from perfect: the halves are on different notes, separated by a tritone:

EX. 41

The exposition expresses this central duality in a brilliantly contrived way. The basic set and its "accompanying melody"—a different rhythmic formulation of the row in a transposed inversion—are imitated at a distance of two bars by a double canon by inversion. The eleventh and twelfth notes of each row are treated as the first and second of the next. This makes for a complex dovetailing of the lines into the ensuing micro-section—which will be the attempted symmetrical retrograde—but it means that immediately the symmetry of the intervallic processions of each half of the exposition is going to be disturbed. Moreover, since the canon is at a two-bar distance, the *proposta* will be attempting its backward movement while the *risposta* is still completing its forward movement. Here too balance will be upset and a tension between the lines created. We have spoken of the attempted retrograde that follows the playing out of each row here: it is "attempted" in the sense that it is far from perfect, either rhythmically or notationally: the order of the notes is somewhat scrambled (though they do move roughly backwards), and the rhythm, being in fact completely altered, is inconsistent with ideal retrograde movement. The whole of the *proposta* as it appears in the exposition is given as follows:

EX. 42

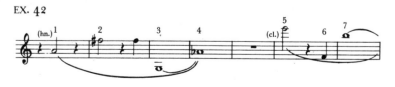

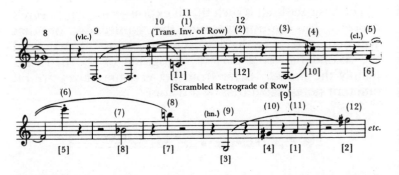

The instrumentation used here and in the other lines clearly enhances one's aural perception of the "retrograde": it will be seen in Ex. 42 that the instruments are used in their reverse order in the second half. Technically this slightly scrambled retrograde is achieved without any offence to the precepts of strict twelve-tonalism: for the properties of the row are such that if it is inverted, and if the first two notes of the inversion are made to coincide with the last two notes of the original series, then the inversion will inevitably return the notes of the original series in a slightly scrambled reverse order.

On many counts, then, this exposition's search for symmetry and balance is defeated; it is also defeated by the codetta-like passage for the "accompanying" line and its canonic partner, and further still by the fact that in the retrograde second half these "accompanying" voices transmit the row—or its inversions or transpositions—more than once, unlike the first half. Now this "retrograde" occurs at the point in the exposition where the second group would normally appear—but this is an important link with the tradition, for the asymmetrical retrograde creates tension and the need for further sections in which to attempt to find harmony and balance, in a way that has important parallels with the traditional function of disparate thematic groups.

The development similarly seeks a bi-unity of canonic forms and extension by retrograde motion. In the first half two voices use the row in its original sequence, though transposed, and the other two use it in transposed inversions. As in the exposition, the voices move in canonic pairs, the following voice in each pair turning upside down what the leading voice has played. The scoring once again clarifies these canons, as it did in the exposition, by the use of certain timbres in the *proposta* that are repeated at the corresponding points in the *risposta*. The four lines share a common rhythm, so that together they make a four-part rhythmic canon. The total reversal begins in bar 35.

It is an unorthodox trait of this development that it exhibits a high degree of symmetry. A notable exception to this general characteristic of the development is the omission by the first canon, in both *proposta* and *risposta*, of the final note (B flat) of its series; this is technically explained only by saying that the note is used to start the ensuing retrograde and that the note is therefore shared by both canons—in the same way that overlapping had occurred in the exposition. What needs to be understood about this generally symmetrical development is that it is (a) not an independent, self-contained section, as is emphasised by its soon being swept aside by the onrush of the recapitulation; and (b) its brevity and relatively uncomplex and homogeneous texture is insufficient to offer an adequate "answer" to the longer and more diverse and intricate exposition: a more satisfactory solution to the symphony's problem—the struggle between Symmetry and Asymmetry—will have to be forthcoming.

But this is nevertheless a real glimpse of the final dénouement, in a way that is not uncommon in the tradition of the symphony; what is uncommon is that it should occupy the development. The recapitulation begins on the last quaver of bar 42. Conventionally, it is varied— most of all in the principal voices, which undergo modifications of rhythm, dynamics, and line through having their component notes moved into different octaves. In other words, the recapitulation brings back the exposition with its original pitch-classes: the effect is of a modulation back into the tonic, but the tensions of imbalance still remain very much in evidence.

Just as the first movement tried to find and unify the perfect mirror forms of canon by inversion and retrograde repetition, so in the second movement each variation makes a greater or lesser attempt to do the same, and similarly has varying degrees of success. As is customary in a symphony, the movement—the finale—begins with the knowledge of the preceding efforts of the symphony, so to speak, and begins therefore that much closer to the sought-for ideal. It exhibits on the whole a higher degree of the kind of balance that is the goal of the symphony, than did the first movement. But the ideal mirror forms are not attained until the end; each section has some greater or lesser "fault", which calls for a renewed attempt and so propels the music on into the next variation.

The theme itself is a transposed inversion of the basic set of the first movement. At its centre-point the theme begins a rhythmic and melodic retrograde of its first half—but as in the original this is imperfect, owing to the fact that the two halves are removed from each other by the interval of a tritone and thus occur on different notes; and canon is virtually non-existent.

Variation I has a high degree of mirror-form integration, but balance is upset and tension created by a lack of synchronization between the two double canons, which begin their backward movement at the distance of half a bar from each other.

Variation II has a very slight canon, but its major disrupting feature is that the first horn refuses to submit to the rigours of retrograde motion; instead it continues to expand thematically and dynamically throughout. This is achieved technically by its consistent alternation between two differently transposed inversions of the series—a kind of mixing of the two rows.

Variation III is ostensibly perfect, but on close attention it reveals a subtle and important "flaw": an extra piece of a row is "tagged on" to the end of the first half (i.e. just before the start of the retrograde), or in other words is inserted into the middle of the variation, and appears both forwards and then immediately backwards. The notes of this insertion are deployed canonically in a very unusual way. There are eight notes in all in this insertion, taken from the middle of a transposed inversion of the row; they are used by two canonic voices, which begin in the centre of this row and move outwards in opposite directions along it. This whole procedure has little to do with the goal of the symphony; in terms of the symphony's concern for perfect symmetry and balance it is an "ungainly" melodic interpolation and as such is a symbolic "imperfection": the perfect mirror forms sought for must be attained without this kind of "compromise".

Variation IV uses a curious, mosaic-like retrograde second half which in terms of the ideal is inadequate. In this retrograde the first half is returned backwards mainly in the sense that melodic cells from it are made to follow each other in reverse order; in other words the first half is taken as consisting of a series of small units—roughly corresponding to bars—which in the second half are placed in reverse order, so that the unit that appeared first in the first half, appears last in the second. Hence this is a compromise with both forward and backward motion.

Variation V has retrograde only minimally—not in its totality, but only in that its ostinato horn figure contains within itself its own retrograde movement:

EX. 43

Instead of anything that can realistically be described as a retrograde second half in the variation, there is just straight-forward repetition, beginning in the middle of bar 60, with another embryonic repetition beginning in bar 65. Variation VI has a deflecting horn on the same principle as Variation II: it also combines two forms of inversions of the series but adds to this expanding melodic tendency a rhythmic freedom as well.

Variation VII at last achieves a perfect bi-union of mirror forms in a complex and expansive (*etwas breiter*) way. Here, finally, double canon by inversion, and retrograde repetition find their perfect form and coexistence. The fairly high dynamic level of this variation, and its broadness—continually expanding further into moments of deceleration—is in keeping with the nature of traditional symphonic apotheosis, or at least resolution. After this the coda can afford to be relaxed, easy, and extremely simple: in these particulars it has links with tradition, too. The relaxation allows a freer borrowing from other (transposed) inversions of the basic set, a freer mixture than hitherto in the symphony, and it allows flexibility in the tempo. It is also no longer preoccupied with canon: it is all simplicity: duality has been conquered. But perhaps its most striking feature is its perfect retrograde motion and total symmetry, aurally apprehended without any difficulty and striking on paper:[3]

EX. 44

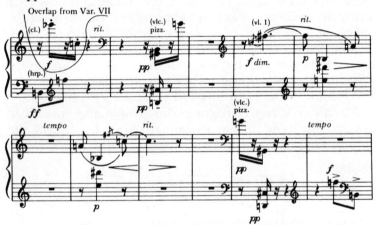

The movement as a whole also reflects the preoccupation with retrograde motion: the coda has affinities with the Thema, and of the other sections Variation VI has clear affinities with Variation II (both have, for instance, a wayward, melodically expanding horn part), Variations V and III have a toccata-like movement, Variations VII and I are more nearly like each other than they are like any other variation (partly because they are the only double canons). Variation IV thus is the centre; and its compromise with forward and backward movement is therefore significant and apt: it tends to emphasize the equivocal position of the variation, caught as it is between forward movement and backward movement. The first movement of course has this kind of broadly forward-and-backward-moving structure as well; but this second movement, which has not to submit to the rigours of recapitulation as does the first, is thus *free* to approach closer to the mirror ideal of the symphony in its total structure than is the first. This too is appropriate and traditional for a finale.

We see, then, that a work that in a technical sense "implies" monism may nevertheless find means for going beyond it. Webern achieves this by bringing about, at all levels from the most fundamentally generative (the row) to the most superstructural, a profound antithesis of Symmetry and Asymmetry. Roberto Gerhard shows another way. His First Symphony (not to be confused with the earlier Pedrell Symphony which is not numbered) incarnates an essential antinomy of *Movement* and *Stasis*.

As has already been mentioned in a different connection (in Chapter 3), Gerhard here uses the total serial field: from the basic twelve-note series he derives correlated proportional sets which control the work in its manifold parameters and which articulate its form in terms of what he calls superordinate time-levels. These levels, or layers, says Gerhard,

> open up fan-wise, each articulating itself within its proper range, and contributing (as a whole) to the articulation of the next higher level, where it becomes simply a member of the superordinate structure; and so forth, up to the highest level which is the whole, in the light of which the parts achieve their proper meaning.[4]

The work is monistic in the sense that the contrasts between divisions—whether on the smallest scale, i.e. the lowest superordinate level, or on the larger, i.e. the higher superordinate levels, such as involve entire movements—do not aspire thematically to the status of entities which "have to bear a destiny of their own", but are contrasts only within the given unity of the tone-row and its correlated proportional sets. Gerhard's total serialism, bringing about form that "as a whole can develop and regulate itself *truly from within*, since its growth will be directed step by step and at all superordinate time levels by the steering operations of the time-set"[5] leads to music that is fundamentally monistic, controlled as it is by a single principle at least as emphatically dominating as a *cantus firmus* in a medieval motet, or a subject in a Bach fugue, where "the entire potential development ... is implicit in the subject."[6]

Yet like Webern (and indeed also like Hamilton and Goehr), Gerhard manages to suggest a powerful dualism *within* the monistic technique. He does this by manifesting two seemingly contradictory states in the music, one associated with movement and rhythm, the other with the stasis that is the suspension of all movement: these become, as we shall see, analogues of, on the one hand, a physical and temporal condition, and on the other, a spiritual, or metaphysical condition. Although these antitheses cannot of course in any simple sense exist simultaneously, their relationship is nevertheless—or rather, precisely *because* of this—profoundly dialectical: the struggle of the symphony is the struggle of the one to attain, or rather to transform itself into, the other. Its struggle, in its striving for what Roman Vlad has called "spiritual summits, and their contemplation in 'privileged moments' ",[7] is one that involves transcendence of those very traits that give the music—at the listener's level of apprehension—its life, its character, its direction, its capacity for growth. These traits are primarily its own propulsive rhythmic life—the "rhythmic forces which seem to embody or to release a train of particular dynamic events" in Vlad's words[8]—and the capacity for melodic formation which is its co-relative in terms of pitch. What this transcendence, this striving towards the metaphysical, means for the work is paradoxically not a denial of the life-forces but precisely an assertion of them. The condition that is sought is thus arrived at through intense rhythmic and melodic assertion; and it is realized in its ultimate and ideal form as silence. The state closest to silence is that in which movement and dynamic level are at their lowest; and the aspiration, by assertion, towards these states provides the dramatic interest of the symphony.

We can follow a pattern, or flux—as the spiritual condition is sought, approached but not fully achieved, and sought again—throughout the whole symphony. Indeed this pattern—broadly a dynamic in which tension mounts and culminates in relaxation—can be shown to be present at every superordinate time-level from the smallest to the largest. The very first page of the score, comprising the first six bars, demonstrates it: the notes of the row are played with a swiftly mounting intensity in which piano rises to fortissimo and the notes follow each other with increasing urgency, involving as they do so more and more regions of the orchestra; after the deafening climax a beat-and-a-half of silence ensues before the next sound is heard:

EX. 45

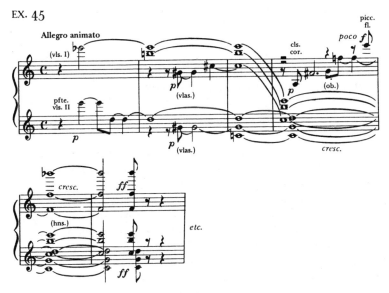

These half-dozen bars demonstrate in a succinct and compelling way the tension–relaxation dynamic that is to be a fundamental preoccupation of the whole symphony; they also reveal the tone-row that is its technical basis. On a higher superordinate time-level, the entire first half of the movement climaxes at cue 15, and in the ensuing ebb of tension the rotating violin ostinato figure that had helped to generate the climax loses its energy as it sinks into a pianissimo and becomes a function no longer of a rhythmic and temporal exigency but of a stillness that is, in its blurred mensurality, almost timeless:

EX. 46

And this makes the point about the symphony's use of ostinato: its use as an intensely physical function is very like its use as precisely the opposite, i.e. as a function of an intense spirituality and inward stillness. The one is the obverse of the other. This means that ostinato, though in a traditional sense "unsymphonic" because of its implications of stasis rather than dynamism, is paradoxically here precisely appropriate to the symphony's central concern.

Still on a higher superordinate time-level, the slow movement is perceived as the relaxation—the greater inwardness that has at the same time a greater, though spiritual, intensity—which has been generated by the first movement as a whole. But the focal point of the whole symphony and its main climax and dramatic turning-point occurs in the region of cue 105 in the last movement. Here a devastating *furioso* climax yields ultimately to intermittent bars of total silence; between these violins and violas move without any of the rhythmic urge that has informed the general movement of the symphony thus far:

EX. 47

At the climax itself an important ostinato, played by the piano—

EX. 48

—is transformed audibly from one which involves forward movement in time to one which is the very suspension of all movement. As the piano emerges from the climax—but not before—the sustaining pedal is depressed with the result that the ostinato figure now being played softly sounds as a chord, without movement; this is especially audible as the piano is, at the moment its pedal is depressed, the only instrument playing.

This section marks the dramatic climax of the symphony, the critical point which has been so long sought but never achieved with this intensity; the point after which things cannot again be the same. The achievement—in the symphony's struggle through "becoming" towards "being" —is decidedly Beethovenian. If all this sounds like verbal sophistry we can invoke the composer's own (reported) words by way of confirmation:

> ... in discussing compositions that are already finished— the *Symphony* or the *String Quartet*, for example—he [i.e. Gerhard] will analyze the structure of certain passages in a peculiarly "dramatic" way: in terms of gestures and trajectories and changes of fortune. He always works now, he says, towards a crisis, or change of fortune, that occurs near the end of the last movement; once this point has been reached, every particle of energy is directed towards the *dénouement*, and it follows that the players must recognize the moment of change and make the dramatic structure clear.[9]

When the rhythmic movement starts up again at cue 118 it does so with greater composure and control, and with less compulsive frenzy. There is an order and symmetry in these pages which is of an altogether new kind; there is even a new light-heartedness and an unmistakable joy. The work moves back to the spiritual state for its conclusion and culminates on a high string-harmonic E, sustained through fourteen bars during which it rises from piano to forte, recedes to pianissimo, and finally trails off into the ultimate state, the silence so earnestly sought.[10]

II

Earlier (Chapter 2) we saw that key might in its symphonic use attain the concreteness of symbol. We saw, for instance, that a work might end in a different key to the one in which it began, and that this ultimate key might be so presented as to appear a "goal" towards which the symphony had striven. Tonality vested with such a significance would add another dimension to the implicit "drama" of symphonic thought. The potential inherent in this symbolic enhancement of tonality is that instead of its being only an addition to the tonal dialectic of a symphony, it might itself become fundamental. Such a change would be more than quantitative. Once the tonal relationships of a symphony are organized such that in principle all its keys are vested with a symbolic character; more precisely, once this outlook is taken as primary, and keys are chosen and organized within and in terms of this fundamental symbolic perspective; then we shall need to take note of a qualitatively different symphonic procedure.

The symphonies of Nielsen are perhaps unique in twentieth-century symphonic thought in making conflict rest upon this qualitatively new method. Of course each symphony of this kind will propose its own symbolic and therefore its own tonal relationships; and only a comprehensive and coherent analysis of any such work will do anything like justice to its procedures. Nevertheless it might be helpful to begin by mentioning summarily some of the relationships which feature prominently in one or more of the symphonies, and the significance with which they are endowed. They include the following: keys tritonally distant from each other appear as antagonists; in such instances, one of these keys usually comes to assume a heroic quality throughout the course of the work and at the end emerges victorious, as the goal to which the struggles of the work have been directed; dramatic use is made of keys semitonally adjacent to a goal-key, whereby it appears that the goal can at this stage be approached only approximately; third-relationships often appear as "equivocal" in character, either in relation to a key with a specific symbolic connotation, or in relation to two keys which are defined as antagonists; keys achieve a characterization that is consistent throughout the symphony, etc. To go beyond this rather superficial enunciation must involve us in some fairly detailed analysis; therefore we shall now proceed to an analysis of, in turn, Nielsen's Third and Fourth Symphonies.[11]

In the Third Symphony (*Sinfonia Espansiva*), A major is at once the tonal goal and symbol of triumph. The first movement begins in D minor. The second group has a clear dramatic function of "oppositeness". Commentators who have used the word "vegetative" to describe this group have specified that function: if the first group (beginning in D minor) characterizes the "expansive" element in the work, the second (beginning in the most remote A flat major) represents the opposite—it seems to "vegetate" by moving within a small compass and being content to "sit" on its tonic or dominant even after each upward movement:

EX. 49

In this context the furious string passages that try to push the group aside may be understood as representatives of the *espansiva* spirit. From the point of view of tonality the exposition and development may superficially appear to have lost touch with traditional practices; at a deeper level, however, they reaffirm these practices by reinterpreting them. As Simpson has observed:

> In the exposition the keys follow a scheme (rising by steps) which, once it has been observed, is as direct as the old tonic-to-dominant trend of the classical exposition: this development is, like the old sonata *Durchführung* much freer in its wanderings from key to key, and is unified by its start and finish in specially selected keys.[12]

In the recapitulation the second group—now in E flat, the furthest point from the symphony's goal—returns before the first: the first group's attempted return fails, as though its capacity for expansion had been temporarily defeated by the development. But when it does return it is extended in order to act also as a kind of coda, and the movement ends with a moment of passing triumph as A major, the goal, is attained.

The slow movement, a Romantically oriented *andante pastorale*, begins in the key (C major) that is a close relative of the tendency that was implicit in the ending of the previous movement—a tendency to slip into A minor. The section moves over a series of rising and quickening pedals a third apart: C, E, G, B, flat, D, F, ... but then, instead of the expected A, the centre is deflected a semitone away to B flat, and from there moves to E flat, once again the very antithesis of the final goal. Yet paradoxically this region, like the E flat second-group section of the first movement's recapitulation (and by analogy the corresponding A flat section in the exposition), is an area of calm to which is given a real human warmth by the addition of wordless soprano and baritone soloists. The movement ends in E flat. The scherzo movement, with a Brahmsian allegretto indication, is set in a kind of sonata form. The movement is in C sharp minor; the second subject is in G major; the tritonal polarity of the groups in the first movement is thus reasserted, in other terms. The movement's central key of C sharp minor is, in the tonal context of the symphony, a somewhat indecisive area: this seems to be the point. And the indecisiveness becomes more obvious when it is understood that since a good deal of the first subject is in B major, and since the second is in G major, they assert poles that are acoustically an equal distance from the idyllic E flat of the previous movement—and, moreover, an equal distance, though significantly a smaller one, from the goal key of the symphony! The development has to free itself of E flat before establishing D major; it then falls back into C sharp minor for the recapitulation. This is condensed: the second subject is now absorbed into the first. The movement ends in C sharp—significantly the only movement to end in its original key. But D major has been found, and it is on this assumption that the finale begins.

Just as the first movement went from D minor to an unstable A major, so this sonata-form moves from a closer point, D major, to a secure A major. The second group enters in B flat minor and soon changes to F sharp minor; these keys are an equidistant third away from the first group's D, and they thus reflect similar equivocations in the scherzo. The movement's antitheses are basically the same symbols as those in the first movement—though their relationship has of course not remained static. The main chorale-like theme of the finale, embodying with new confidence the *espansiva* spirit of the first group of the first movement, has now a tendency to take its opposite into itself: notice its characteristic lingering on the dominant, a trait which belonged to the "vegetative" second group of the first movement:

EX. 50

The second subject, too, has clear motivic affinities with the first:

EX. 51

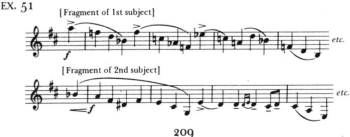

But it still expresses the dominant fixation, a demurring, declining gesture—the opposite of *espansiva*—with which it makes endless play when it returns in B flat major in the recapitulation. This reprise of the second subject—before the first, and again for obvious dramatic reasons—occurs just after the great E major climax of the development; thus again the "vegetative" spirit stresses the opposite pole, just as it did, say, in the E flat recapitulation of the first movement, and in the E flat episode of the andante—for E flat bears the same relation to the goal A of the symphony, as B flat does to E, the dominant of the goal key. But the point has now been reached where reconciliation, and the achievement of the A major goal, are possible: the goal tonality is indeed affirmed, and the first subject *absorbs* the second into itself:

EX. 52

[Quotation from 2nd subject]

The Fourth Symphony (*The Inextinguishable*) is a still clearer demonstration of the way in which Nielsen's thorough-going key symbolism extended and revitalized the symphonic use of tonality. The work's four movements are continuous. The first group opens the allegro with a hellish violence, destructive of tonal security: two tonal centres are thrown together (C in the strings and D in the woodwind), and the tritone is ominously present both vertically and horizontally. The second group, in a calm A major, is an intense contrast; and its key bears an orthodox relation to the D of the first group. The clarinet's long, smooth cantilena is soon interrupted as the alien tritonal relation—E flat—almost succeeds in establishing A flat minor. But the Will to Life—which is what the composer said the music attempted to express—prevails and instead the orchestra suddenly gives out, in a *fortissimo* and *risoluto* E major, a clipped version of the second group. It is a brief moment of triumph—and the first glimpse of the goal tonality of the symphony. But victory is not so easily won, and E major is lost in the fifth bar. The development is full combat, with sudden tonal movements, and with the "positive" (second-group) elements striving to control the other (first-group) elements and to establish E major. Towards the end of the development the second group finds a welcome stability in C major, and we are led to believe that something has been gained. But this is too easy: and C, we remember, was originally associated with the first group. Without warning, the demoniacal first group sweeps over all. Before the end of the recapitulation the music finds itself within the perimeter of E major, and gathers strength to heave itself into that key and into a full-blooded statement of the second group. As if exhausted by the effort, the music sinks into a diminuendo.

But some respite has been won: this takes the form of a graceful allegretto movement, another "scherzo" of the Brahmsian kind, in the nearly related G major. The scoring is fastidious; it is predominantly for woodwinds, who were the bringers of the peace of the second group of the first movement. With the slow movement, non-being suddenly, frighteningly, annihilates all. We are back with the struggle to establish E major; this is what the early writhing string line tries to do, despite its macabre timpani and pizzicato accompaniment. The free string polyphony that this section soon attains is in striking contrast to the previous woodwind movement with its homophony and period structures. E major is indeed achieved after a while, and the new section breaks upon the scene with wonderful simplicity; but before long E major again disappears, and as the "dangerous" calm of C major is found a piercing ostinato screech introduces a destructive "developmental" section. This ostinato figure is a derivative of the opening theme of the movement, and after a fugal discourse it locks in contrapuntal battle with the second theme. Tension builds until the second theme can find an ostinato equal to that of the first theme, whereupon E major bursts forth and imposes a sudden stability. There is no reprise: the themes are spent, and as odd motives from them whirl about the goal tonality is once more mislaid.

The finale opens with a thematic complex of beautiful simplicity and confidence, in a mixolydian A major: it is the first of the three "conflict" movements to begin with the "Life" element in the work, and not with its opposite. The second group this time unleashes the chaos, and does so with vengeance. The startling section of the group for solo timpani bears in the score the composer's instruction that both timpanists maintain a menacing character, even in piano sections. The tritone is again prominent. In the midst of this fury there arise hints of the main subject; at these suggestions the music restores calm with a huge *glorioso* placation in A major, bringing to an end what may be seen as the exposition. The development deploys temporarily deflated motives from the second subject and repeated-note figures from previous movements, until quiet canonic musings with the first subject introduce the recapitulation. This is in B major—the dominant of the goal key—and before long there are premonitions of a return of the once triumphant "Life" theme of the first movement. Yet the music darkens again: B major drops to minor, and soon the drums are pounding out their destruction. Between them the drums create D minor—the key of the very beginning of the work. The first subject of the finale falls away under this primitive fury, but the first movement's "Life" theme holds grimly on. A sudden outburst of the furious second group temporarily drives away all before it; but the first "Life" theme and E major have been prepared, and with a mighty ejaculation call everything to instant order: even the frenzied quavers of the second group are quelled, being turned into ostinato violin accompaniment, and the symphony ends triumphantly.

NOTES

[1] i.e. "Shape" and "Texture": the terms were frequently used by Tovey, as has already been noted.

[2] From the sleeve-notes provided by the composer for the Argo recording of the work in 1967.

[3] Of course, though we have spoken of perfect retrograde in connection with the last two sections, it must be understood that grace-notes are treated differently, with melodic considerations foremost; thus for instance [musical notation] would in retrograde become [musical notation] and not [musical notation]

[4] *The Score*, September 1956, p. 70.

[5] *ibid.*, p. 63. The italics are mine.

[6] Furtwängler, Wilhelm; *op.cit.*, p. 29.

[7] "My first impressions of Roberto Gerhard's music', *The Score*, September 1956, p. 31.

[8] *ibid.*, p. 29.

[9] Glock, William; "Comment", *The Score*, September 1956, pp. 6–7.

[10] It is interesting to observe that E is the goal-tone of the symphony, and a kind of symbol of achievement. It appears at moments of high achievement in the work—the end of the first movement, at the end of the second movement, and at significant points in the dénouement of the last (E is the first note introduced over the piano ostinato after the furioso climax, when in the first violins it leads off the pianissimo string-tremolo reiteration of all the notes in the series; it is also the first note to be heard after each of four General Pauses, and of course it is the last note of the symphony). Its use in this way, though, is symbolic rather than anything which could meaningfully be called a tonal centre.

[11] In this discussion of Nielsen's symphonies I am indebted to Robert Simpson's excellent functional harmonic analyses in his *Carl Nielsen: Symphonist.*

[12] *op. cit.*, pp. 51–52.

Epilogue

The continued productivity in that field of composition called symphony—despite the repeated pronouncements about its death or irrelevancy—is an interesting fact of the musical life of the twentieth century. It is also one that raises explicit questions about the relationship of present to past in a traditional musical field, and raises them at least as emphatically as composition in any other single comparable field. Almost invariably these questions are overlooked by commentators; this would be at least understandable if it were obviously true (which it isn't) that all symphonies written in our century had been left quite untouched by contemporary developments in music and were thus totally anomalous, or that they had all so radically broken free of tradition that their only connection with older symphonies was in their use of the name, and the questions raised were thus more superficial ones of semantics. Doubtless there are symphonies which are accurately characterized by one or other of these extreme positions; but clearly the bulk of symphonic composition from Mahler onwards falls somewhere in between, and the questions still loom large.

It is to these questions that our study has hoped to suggest means of approach and answer. In pursuing the symphonic tradition from its earliest meaningful beginnings to the present time, we have found the symphony capable of extraordinary survival. We have seen how it may be transmitted in diverse ways into widely diverse idioms. Frequently we have surprised ourselves by discovering a fundamentally symphonic essence where all surface indications were strongly against our ever doing so; and in each such case we have uncovered a method of profound

214

reinterpretation of the symphonic idea. It is not our task here to predict whether or not the symphony will continue to survive, or indeed to argue whether this survival is necessary or even desirable. What has become clear, however, is that the symphony can, if required to do so, rethink a number of its basic tenets in terms appropriate to highly contemporary idioms. And the proven resilience of the symphonic principle—a function of the human needs it fulfills—should put us on our guard against any too glib prediction, or diagnosis, of its death.

Select Bibliography

ABRAHAM, GERALD; *Eight Soviet Composers*, London 1943.

ABRAHAM, GERALD; *A Hundred Years of Music*, London (rev.) 1964.

ABRAHAM, GERALD; *On Russian Music*, London 1939.

ABRAHAM, GERALD (ed.); *Schubert: a Symposium*, London 1946.

ABRAHAM, GERALD (ed.); *Schumann: a Symposium*, London 1952.

ABRAHAM, GERALD (ed.); *Sibelius: a Symposium*, London 1952.

ABRAHAM, GERALD; *Studies in Russian Music*, London 1935.

ABRAHAM, GERALD (ed.); *Tchaikovsky: a Symposium*, London 1945.

AUSTIN, WILLIAM; *Music in the Twentieth Century*, New York 1966.

BALLANTINE, CHRISTOPHER; "Beethoven, Hegel and Marx", *Music Review*, Vol. 33, No. 1, Feb. 1972, pp. 34–46.

BARZUN, JACQUES; *Berlioz and the Romantic Century*, 2 vols., London 1951.

BEKKER, PAUL; *Beethoven*, London 1925.

BERRY, WALLACE; *Form in Music*, Englewood Cliffs, New Jersey 1966.

BLUME, FRIEDRICH; *Classic and Romantic Music*, London 1972.

CARDUS, NEVILLE; *Gustav Mahler: his Mind and his Music*, Vol. 1, London 1965.

CARNER, MOSCO; "A Beethoven movement and its successors", *Music and Letters*, Vol. 20, 1939, pp. 281–291.

CHERNIAVSKY, DAVID; "Germ motives in Sibelius", *Music and Letters*, Vol. 23, No. 1, January 1942, pp. 1–9.

CLAPHAM, JOHN; *Antonin Dvořák: Musician and Craftsman*, London 1966.

COKER, WILSON; *Musical Meaning: A Theoretical Introduction to Musical Aestheitcs*, New York 1972.

COLLAER, PAUL; *A History of Modern Music* (tr. Sally Abeles), Cleveland 1961.

COLLES, H. C.; *Symphony and Drama, 1850–1900* (*Oxford History of Music*, Vol. VII), London 1934.

COOPER, MARTIN (ed.); *The Modern Age: 1890–1960* (*New Oxford History of Music*, Vol. X), London 1974.

CROCKER, RICHARD L.; *A History of Musical Style*, New York 1966.

CUYLER, LOUISE; *The Symphony*, New York 1973.

DANNREUTHER, EDWARD; *The Romantic Period* (*Oxford History of Music*, Vol. VI), London 1934.

DEL MAR, NORMAN; *Richard Strauss: a Critical Commentary on his Life and Work*, 2 Vols., London 1962.

DICKINSON, A. E. F.; *Vaughan Williams*, London 1963.

DOERNBERG, ERWIN; *The Life and Symphonies of Anton Bruckner*, London 1960.

EINSTEIN, ALFRED; *Mozart: His Character his Work* (tr. Arthur Mendel and Nathan Broder), London 1946.

EINSTEIN, ALFRED; *Music in the Romantic Era*, London 1947.

ENGELSMANN, WALTER; "Beethoven and the creative law of symphonic art", *Musical Quarterly*, Vol. 23, 1937, pp. 56–63.

EVANS, EDWIN; *Handbook to the Choral and Orchestral Works of Brahms*, Vols. 2 and 3, London 1936.

EVANS, PETER; "Martinů the Symphonist", *Tempo*, 55/56, 1960, pp. 19–33.

FRIEDHEIM, PHILIP; "The relationship between tonality and musical structure", *Music Review*, February 1966, Vol. 27, No. 1, pp. 44–54.

FURTWÄNGLER, WILHELM; *Concerning Music* (tr. L. J. Lawrence), London 1953.

GEORGE, GRAHAM; *Tonality and Musical Structure*, London 1970 .

GERHARD, ROBERTO; "Developments in twelve-tone technique", *The Score*, September 1956, pp. 61–72.

GROUT, DONALD JAY; *A History of Western Music*, London 1962.

GROVE, GEORGE; *Beethoven and his Nine Symphonies*, London 1896.

HADOW, HENRY; *Sonata Form*, London N. D.

HAGGIN, B. H.; *A Book of the Symphony*, London 1937.

HARTOG, HOWARD (ed.); *European Music in the Twentieth Century*, London (rev.) 1961.

HILL, RALPH (ed.); *The Symphony*, London 1952.

HOPKINS, ANTHONY; *Talking about Symphonies*, London 1961.

KELLER, HANS; "Sonata and symphony today", *Music Review*, May 1961, Vol. 22, No. 2, p. 172.

KEMP, IAN (ed.); *Michael Tippett: a Symposium on his Sixtieth Birthday*, London 1965.

KOLNEDER, WALTER; *Anton Webern: An Introduction to his Works* (tr. Humphrey Searle), London 1968.

KRAUSE, ERNST; *Richard Strauss: the Man and his Work* (tr. John Coombs), London 1964.

LAMBERT, CONSTANT; *Music Ho!*, London (rev.) 1937.

LANG, PAUL HENRY; *Music in Western Civilisation*, London 1941.

LATHAM, PETER; *Brahms* ("The Master Musicians" series), London 1962.

LAYTON, ROBERT; *Sibelius* ("The Master Musicians" series), London 1965.

LAYTON, ROBERT; *Britain, Scandinavia and the Netherlands* (*Twentieth Century Composers*, Vol. 3), London 1972.

LEE, E. MARKHAM; *The Story of the Symphony*, London 1916.

LEICHTENTRITT, HUGO; *Musical Form*, Cambridge, Massachusetts 1951.

MACHLIS, JOSEPH; *Introduction to Contemporary Music*, London 1963.

MELLERS, WILFRED, and HARMAN, ALEC; *Man and His Music*, London 1962.

MELLERS, WILFRED; *Music in a New Found Land*, London 1964.

MELLERS, WILFRED; *Studies in Contemporary Music*, London 1947.

MITCHELL, DONALD; *Gustav Mahler: the Early Years*, London 1958.

MITCHELL, DONALD; *Gustav Mahler: the Wunderhorn Years*, London 1975.

NESTYEV, ISRAEL; *Prokofiev* (tr. Florence Jonas), New York 1960.

NEWLIN, DIKA; *Bruckner, Mahler, Schoenberg*, New York 1947.

OTTAWAY, HUGH; "Vaughan Williams and the symphonic epilogue", *Musical Opinion*, Vol. 79, December 1955, pp. 145–147.

PARMET, SIMON; *The Symphonies of Sibelius* (tr. K. A. Hart), London 1959.

RAUCHHAUPT, URSULA VON (ed.); *The Symphony*, London 1973.

REDLICH, HANS; *Bruckner and Mahler*, London 1963.

RETI, RUDOLPH; *The Thematic Process in Music*, London 1961.

RIEZLER, WALTER: *Beethoven* (tr. G. D. H. Pidcock), London 1938.

ROBBINS LANDON, H. C.; *The Symphonies of Joseph Haydn*, London 1955.

ROSEN, CHARLES; *The Classical Style*, London 1971.

ROSEN, CHARLES; *Arnold Schoenberg*, London 1976.

ŠAFRÁNEK, MILOŠ; *Bohuslav Martinů: His Life and Works* (tr. Roberta Finlayson-Samsourova), London 1962.

SAINT-FOIX, G. DE; *The Symphonies of Mozart* (tr. L. Orrey), London 1947.

SALAZAR, ADOLFO; *Music in Our Time* (tr. I. Pope), New York 1946.

SALZMAN, ERIC; *Twentieth-Century Music: an Introduction*, Englewood Cliffs, New Jersey 1967.

SCHERCHEN, HERMANN; *The Nature of Music* (tr. William Mann), London 1950.

SCHOENBERG, ARNOLD; *Fundamentals of Musical Composition*, London 1967.

SEARLE, HUMPHREY, and LAYTON, ROBERT; *Britain, Scandinavia and the Netherlands* (*Twentieth Century Composers*, Vol. 3), London 1972.

SIMPSON, ROBERT; *Carl Nielsen: Symphonist*, London 1952.

SIMPSON, ROBERT; *The Essence of Bruckner*, London 1967.

SIMPSON, ROBERT (ed.); *The Symphony*, 2 vols., London 1966.

SPINK, IAN; *An Historical Approach to Musical Form*, London 1967.

STEIN, ERWIN; *Orpheus in New Guises*, London 1953.

STERNFELD, F. W.(ed.); *Music in the Modern Age (A History of Western Music*, Vol. V), London 1973.

STUCKENSCHMIDT, HANS; *Arnold Schoenberg* (tr. E. T. Roberts and H. Searle), London 1959.

STUCKENSCHMIDT, HANS; *Germany and Central Europe (Twentieth Century Composers*, Vol. 2), London 1970.

THOMSON, VIRGIL; *American Music since 1910 (Twentieth Century Composers*, Vol. 1), London 1971.

TOVEY, DONALD FRANCIS; *Beethoven*, London 1944.

TOVEY, DONALD FRANCIS; *Essays in Musical Analysis*, 6 vols., London 1935-9.

TOVEY, DONALD FRANCIS; *A Musician Talks*, 2 vols., London 1941.

ULRICH, HOMER; *Symphonic Music: its Evolution since the Renaissance*, New York 1952.

VLAD, ROMAN; "My first Impressions of Roberto Gerhard's music", *The Score*, September 1956, pp. 27-34.

WALKER, ALAN; *A Study in Musical Analysis*, London 1962.

WALKER, ALAN (ed.); *Franz Liszt: The Man and his Music*, London 1970.

WEINGARTNER, FELIX; *The Symphony since Beethoven* (tr. A. Bles), London N. D.

WERNER, ERIC; *Mendelssohn: a New Image of the Composer and his Age* (tr. Dika Newlin), New York 1963.

YOUNG, PERCY M.; *Symphony*, London 1957.

Index